Weighing.  cales vary greatly and it _____ eight loss (or gain!) on _____ a copy of Chart 4 on p_____ /e found it best to weigh ~~everyone as they came in~~. It encouraged the group to strip ready for the exercises and prevented us from standing around waiting until everyone had arrived. Latecomers should weigh after the exercises have finished. Weigh one another. This is not only to prevent cheating; it is quite difficult to get an accurate reading when the scales are read from a height.

If you are about to have or actually have your monthly period, your weight may be up as much as 5 lb (2·5 kg). Carry on as usual; it is such a pleasure to lose so much the following week! Check the weight guide for your age, height and bone structure (pp. 55–6).

Measuring. This should be done at the beginning and end of each six weeks' course. You cannot lose inches as quickly as you can lose pounds. Measure your bust, waist, hips, and top of leg, all at their thickest part, making sure not to pinch the flesh.

Measure your height without shoes, back against the wall, heels on the floor, and with a book or ruler on your head.

To check your bone structure measure your wrist. Approximately, large bones give a $6\frac{2}{3}''$ (17 cm) wrist measurement, medium bones $6\frac{1}{3}''$ (16 cm) and small bones 6″ (15 cm). A large bone structure adds about 5 lb (2·5 kg) to the ideal weight and small bone structure deducts 5 lb (2·5 kg).

Although you inherit your basic body framework you do not inherit a fat figure. If, however, you are overweight, you do inherit a tendency for the fat to accumulate in particular areas of the body. In some people the excess fat is evenly distributed but for others it settles in the bust, hips, legs, thighs or waist.

If you want to reduce certain areas of the body, wrap a large thin plastic bag next to the skin round the offending part. Do your exercises with it on under your Slimnastics clothes. This method has been used by dancers all over the world with great success. For it to be most effective you really need to use it every day.

Fat is mostly water. The plastic causes the area to perspire more profusely, and the exercise increases the blood supply and this removes the waste products more efficiently. Banging the fat parts on the floor or a wall, and slapping them with the hand, breaks down the fatty tissue.

You may have to wrap a bandage round the edges of the plastic to soak up the moisture. After removing the plastic bag it is important to rub yourselves down with a towel and wash the area with cold water to close the pores. After a wash, shower or bath, rub olive oil on the skin to keep it elastic and replace the natural oils. Your exercises are also strengthening the muscles so you will be left with a firmer, more shapely and less bulky area.

If you are controlling your weight and doing the exercises regularly you will have lost inches by the end of a six weeks' course.

Taking Charge of a Group

To give you confidence we thought you might be interested to hear how Diana Lamplugh got on and her reactions with her first class. Although this was in her home, her experience may help you in running a group anywhere.

When it actually came to the point (Diana says) I was scared stiff. I soon realized it was not going to be as easy as I had thought.

My first difficulty was whom to ask to join me. Some of my friends had superb figures, others were far too thin, and others really needed to slim. Pamela insisted that everyone would benefit from the course whatever their figure at the start; she said thin ones would build up their muscles and curves, near perfect ones would tone up their muscles and increase their sparkle, and the overweight would show remarkable improvement. But how on earth could I say to my plump friends, 'Come and slim with me'! In the event I need not have worried. Instead of being insulted, everyone was delighted when I tentatively mentioned the idea. Before I knew where I was, my group was over-full with enthusiastic women, some of whom I had never met before.

That was the first hurdle over. Now the actual classes. I grew cold with fright. I whittled the numbers down to six as that seemed the right number for the room, especially as nearly everyone had children (another headache – would they tear the place apart?). We all decided that the best time to meet was from 2 to 3 p.m. Most of our mornings were busy – some of us were working part time, others had babies and other commitments apart from housework, and most had children to fetch from school. We all had busy lives and felt we would only keep it up for six weeks if we knew that we could start on time, work hard for an hour, collapse, have a cup of tea, and leave on time, staying to chat if we felt inclined but otherwise able to dash away and not feel guilty.

So far so good. As the first Tuesday approached I really panicked. I read and re-read the course and simply prayed that everyone would take it seriously. Again I need not have worried. They all wanted to succeed, they all genuinely wanted to make the effort. We all weighed immediately, no one showed any embarrassment, but quite a number of us gasped with horror at the reading on the scales. We read each other's weights and took each other's measurements not only to make sure they were correct but also to see that no one cheated! We cleared the room, turned on the music and started the exercises. At the beginning we felt extremely foolish marching together and thinking what an odd sight we must make, especially as the children lined up and stood stock still, gaping in awe. Before a few minutes were up we had started to enjoy ourselves; the younger babies went back to playing with bricks or sat still to watch, and the older four to five year olds were soon joining in with enthusiasm and vying with their mothers as to who could do best. The children won every time!

I found it surprisingly easy to direct the exercises although I was doing them myself. I kept the text beside me all the time. I was rather inclined to cheat at first, cutting down the number of times and starting the next exercise when I got tired myself. I realized this when one week I hurt my leg and had to sit down just telling everyone what to do. They all complained what a hard taskmaster I had become! We came to the conclusion that it was best either to take turns to lead or to refer to exercises oneself and just try to keep in time with others.

Amazingly no one missed a week. No one forgot to bring their equipment, which we found surprisingly easy to obtain and make, and great fun to use. Pamela still assured us it would not make enormous muscles. The first week no one lost much weight and we were all a little discouraged; however, once the weights started going down the competition was fast and furious. Very few of us will ever have sugar again. Not having a professional amongst us, we were completely thrown off balance if a stranger came to watch. Unless people joined in, they were carefully locked out. We found the garden in the sun too hot but marvellous on coolish, sunny days. We were surprised how well we felt immediately after our class. Nearly everyone did the recommended homework exercises for five minutes a day. I am told that even husbands joined in and thoroughly enjoyed themselves. My husband thought I was a bit of a nut, but I was given a fabulous evening suit which I could never have worn before, and certainly we all gained in confidence and spirit.

2. Controlling Your Weight

It is a plain and simple fact that being overweight is almost always due to too much food of the wrong type for your own particular needs. (It is also due to hormonal effects of pregnancy, breast feeding and oral contraception, as well as some medical conditions.) We ask all members of our Slimnastics groups to keep an honest record of their daily food intake. By the end of a week it is usually abundantly clear even to themselves where they are going wrong. These surveys among our groups cover a wide cross-section of women and include most age groups and occupations. We have based this chapter on medical and professional dietetic advice that we have been given.

First let us examine the different food elements which make up our daily diet and keep us alive and healthy. These are proteins, fats, carbohydrates, vitamins, minerals and water.

The Elements of Food

Proteins are found in meat (including offal), fish (including shell fish), eggs, cheese, milk and some vegetable sources, especially oatmeal and whole grain cereals. Protein is needed all the time to make good the 'wear and tear' of body tissues in the process of living and an extra amount is needed during the stages of growth, pregnancy and breast feeding.

Fats are found in butter, margarine, meat, eggs, cheese milk and other animal fats and also vegetable oils. The body uses fats to make warmth and although it can do without fats for some time it cannot do so indefinitely.

Carbohydrates are the foods consisting mainly of starch and sugar; for example, flour, bread, cakes, peas, potatoes, rice, honey, jam, sweets, biscuits, cakes, puddings, alcohol. Although carbohydrates usually provide the greatest part of the calories in a normal diet no individual carbohydrate is a dietary necessity.

Vitamins protect the body against infection and disease. They are important for growth, good eyesight, and digestion, and generally aid the body to work efficiently. They are found in fresh food, fruit, vegetables, dairy produce, liver and fish liver oils.

Minerals are essential but most are needed in such minute quantities that no diet would normally be deficient. However, the important minerals to note are:

Salt the average diet contains four or five times as much as is strictly needed.

Iodine this is usually found in the drinking water. In many cases iodine is added to table salt.

Calcium and phosphorus these minerals build up the bones and the teeth. They are found in milk and cheese.

Iron this is necessary for the red cells of the blood. Iron is present in meat, fish, eggs, liver, lentils, split peas, oatmeal, spinach and beans.

Fluorine has been shown to be important for the prevention of caries in teeth.

Water. Water makes up nearly three-quarters of our body weight. Our bodies can last for quite a time without food but cannot survive for long without water.

Calories

Human energy needs are measured in calories. The number of calories required by human beings depends mainly on their size, their age (especially if they are growing), the amount of muscular activity or work done, and the climate in which they live. Some of these calories are used to produce heat, and the rest for internal chemical reactions and bodily processes or in active movements and in actual work done.

Food is the fuel which provides the calories. Ideally the fuel intake should equal the energy output. If the output is more than the fuel intake the body has to find its calories from its own tissues. Carried to extremes this can cause malnutrition and starvation. If the calorie intake is more than the output, the excess is stored in fat and consequently causes overweight.

Much research is being done to discover why some people burn up more calories than others. For example, two friends may say that they both eat exactly the same amount of food, yet one is overweight and the other skinny. The thin girl is probably wasting a lot of calories in producing and giving off a great deal more heat all the time, even when she is asleep. She may be more energetic and restless. The plump friend probably has a more efficient body which wastes fewer calories by giving out less heat in addition to which her body is better insulated by her thicker layer of fat. She is consequently giving her body fuel which it does not need and this is being stored. If she reduces her intake of food she will slowly but surely lose weight. She will also lose weight if she increases her energy output by taking more exercise and stimulating her mind, also by throwing off her phlegmatic attitude and taking a new interest in things around her. In the same way if the skinny friend increases her food intake she will gain weight and she will also gain if she tries to lead a quieter life and take things more calmly.

In order to control our weight it is therefore vital that we should take an honest look at ourselves. We are all very different. Life is unfair but we must live with the facts and turn them to our advantage. In this way we can tackle our weight problems at the source and find our own solution.

Cutting Down the Food Intake

It is quite clear that if you want to cut down your weight you must cut down your intake of food. There are countless recommended diets and aids for weight control. Some are excellent and some are useless. 'Crash' diets are marvellous for losing the few odd pounds but no good in the long run. If you slim hard for a while, then stop and then start again, you upset your metabolism and do more harm than good.

As we have seen, the necessary foods to keep the body alive and healthy are proteins, fats, vitamins, minerals, and water. It is only carbohydrates which can be cut down without doing any harm. It is an interesting fact that primeval man had no problems of overweight. Before man learned to refine sugar he had all he needed from raw fruit and vegetables. We do not suggest that you should cut out carbohydrates altogether, but that they should be kept to a minimum. It is much easier to overeat carbohydrates than any other foods. One can acquire an addiction to sugar, sweets and chocolate. A doctor friend of ours considers that they are the curse of modern society.

We have compiled a list of high carbohydrate foods which should be cut out entirely by anyone who is trying to lose weight, but in fact everyone will benefit by cutting these foods to a minimum. The limited list also applies to the slimmers; if you are under or of average weight you can have as much as you like from this list. The high protein list is for everyone. Do not forget that although you are allowed to eat unlimited butter, for example, you cannot have any bread to eat it on. You will find these lists at the end of the chapter.

If you are aiming to lose weight it will not be easy, at first, to cut down the carbohydrate list. They are nearly all delightful temptations. This is where the Slimnastics group gives you the will and encouragement to continue. Keep the exciting idea in mind that once you have reached your desired weight you can indulge yourself occasionally, provided, of course, that you keep an eye on the scales. Remember too that it is better to eat small regular meals than to starve yourself all day and then overeat at night.

Learning to control your Weight

The first necessity is to check your weight against the chart showing the ideal for your age, height, and bone structure (pp. 55–6). Having determined whether you are under, average or over weight, write out with complete honesty your meals for a week including any snacks and noting any out-of-the-ordinary activities. At the end of the week study the results and see what they reveal. For examples see the chapter on the Five Ages of Women.

Underweight. If you are underweight you may find that you are simply not eating enough. You are burning up more calories than you are putting back and your energy is therefore coming from within the body itself. You can increase the intake of carbohydrates providing you are including enough protein in your diet. Increasing the carbohydrates will automatically step up the fat content because the majority of starchy foods contain a large percentage of fat – for example cakes, biscuits and pies. You should not only try to increase the body fuel but also make a huge effort to decrease the body activity. Try to cultivate a quieter and calmer attitude to life. The Slimnastics exercises will help you to relax.

Average weight. If you are maintaining a good average weight then your body is well adjusted. You have balanced the input and output of calories. Although you may overeat one day, you probably automatically re-adjust your diet the following day. But this should not excuse you from writing out your weekly diet. You may keep an average weight but are you eating as healthily as you could? Does your diet include all the foods groups listed with proteins and fats predominant? Are you including enough vitamins and minerals?

Overweight. However little you may think you are eating, you are still giving the body more fuel than it needs and this is being stored in fat.

In learning to control your weight, the first essential is absolute honesty with yourself. Following the examples on the next few pages, make a completely accurate note of all the food you eat during the first week. When you study this before the next Slimnastics meeting it should be fairly obvious where you are making your mistakes. Use the food lists as a guide and plan your menus for the next few weeks. Each week bring your completed diet sheet to the Slimnastics meeting. You can then discuss your ideas, successes and failures with other members of the group. If you are still not losing enough weight by the end of the third week, keep to the same lists of foods but cut down the quantities further.

As you will now be doing the Slimnastics exercises as well you will be increasing the calorie output at the same time as you are decreasing the calorie intake. It is a fallacy to suppose that exercise increases the appetite to any great extent. In fact the appestat, or appetite control, is at its most efficient when the body is being fully exercised. It is the sedentary worker whose appetite exceeds the body's requirements.

The effort of keeping to a sensible diet becomes easier as the weeks go by, especially with the help of others in the Slimnastics group. When you have reached your ideal weight, you can experiment with some additions from the forbidden list, but weigh yourself each week to watch for any warning increase in weight. If you follow these ideas carefully you will establish for yourself a healthy and balanced diet to suit your own way of life.

**List 1.
Unrestricted**
(as much as you like
for everyone)

All unadulterated meat and offal – lean and fat (no sausages, etc.).

All fish including tinned fish.

Dairy products and eggs – cream, butter, cheese. (No ice-cream. Milk is restricted because it has some carbohydrate.)

Vegetables – asparagus, broccoli, brussels sprouts, cabbage, cauliflower, celery, chicory, cucumber, green beans, lettuce, marrow, mushrooms, onions, radishes, spinach, string beans, tomatoes, turnips and watercress. (No thick sauces – these include carbohydrate.)

Fruits – black and red currants, gooseberries and rhubarb (not cooked in sugar).

Drinks – bouillon, yeast extract.

**List 2.
Restricted
Foods**
(limited quantities for
the overweight)

Milk – about two glassfuls a day, 1 yoghourt (unflavoured).

Vegetables – small amounts allowed of artichokes, carrots, parsnips, pumpkins and peas.

Fruit – one item a day allowed from this list, apple (1), apricots (3), damsons (3), figs (2), greengages (2), grapes (small bunch), ½ grapefruit, cantaloupe melon (1 slice) nuts (handful), orange (1), peach (1), pear (1), pineapple (1 slice), plums (up to 6), or raspberries, strawberries, blackberries or cherries (ordinary serving).

List 3.
High
Carbohydrate
Foods
(strictly forbidden for
the overweight)

No sugar, no jam, honey, syrup or treacle, no marmalade, no sweets or chocolate, no ice-cream, no tinned fruits in syrup.

No baked beans, no bananas, no corn-on-the-cob, no potato, no dried or preserved fruits, no thick soup.

No bread, toast, or rolls, no biscuits, no buns, cakes, no pastries, no puddings, no desserts such as pies, jellies or custards, no breakfast cereals, no spaghetti, macaroni, vermicelli, rice, tapioca, semolina, etc., no sausages, no fried foods.

No fizzy drinks unless they are certified as having no calories.

Alcohol

Low-carbohydrate	High carbohydrate
Whisky, gin, vodka, rum,	Beer of all kinds
martini, dry sherry,	Eggnog and most mixed
dry red, and white	drinks
wines	Sweet wines

This does not give dieters the liberty to rush straight to the whisky bottle! Although so much alcohol is low in carbohydrates it has been discovered that the consumption of alcohol slows down the rate at which the body burns up its surplus fat. Alcohol is converted direct to body heat. This is the job normally carried out by fat, therefore you retain fat. We should cut down our intake of alcohol to a minimum and ideally cut it out altogether.

Coffee and Tea

Cutting down the intake of food is much easier if coffee as well as caffeine in other forms (such as strong tea, chocolate, and some soft drinks) is avoided altogether. It is a great temptation to drink black coffee to allay the pangs of hunger. However, the chemical reaction within the body will result in lowering the blood sugar and a short while later this will make you even more hungry. Decaffeinated coffee will not have the same effect.

Tips for Low-Carbohydrate Diets

Many members of our Slimnastics groups suggested to us some interesting ideas which were helping them keep to their low-carbohydrate diets. We have compiled a list for we felt they might help you too.

(1) Plan your menus one week in advance. Write a careful list and shop as few times as possible. Quick impulse shopping can be a great temptation.

(2) Try to cut unnecessary carbohydrate foods out of your larder altogether. One of our overweight group members who felt she *must* give sweets, biscuits and cakes to the children stuck an unflattering photograph of herself inside the biscuit tin. She lost weight very quickly.

(3) If you find it difficult to cut down on sugar, duplicate every spoonful you take during the day, putting it into a special bowl. When you actually see the amount you eat it may give you quite a surprise.

(4) Do your daily exercises in a figure-revealing swim-suit or leotard in front of a mirror.

(5) Try to eat salads and uncooked food as often as possible. Apart from the fact that foods which can be eaten raw are usually low in carbohydrate it is much more difficult to overeat them.

(6) If you have less food on your plate than everyone else, cut your food small and eat slowly enjoying every mouthful. In this way you will finish your meal at the same time as the others.

(7) Hot drinks are excellent appetite-reducers. It is therefore a good idea to include a cup of hot bouillon or yeast extract with your lunch or supper.

(8) If you are a dedicated nibbler, allow yourself a small piece of cheese, a stick of celery, a raw carrot or a few nuts instead of sweets and biscuits.

Roughage

Roughage is essential for regular bowel action, which clears the body quickly and efficiently of waste products and bacteria. As refined foods these days, for example white sugar and white bread, contain little or no rough-age, doctors recommend that everyone should include in his diet natural foods, for example plenty of green vegetables and if necessary a little bran every day.

3. The Five Ages of Women

We felt it might give you heart and inspiration if we studied some actual case histories from our Slimnastics groups. For the exercises it has been necessary roughly to divide women into five groups and so we have selected a weekly diet sheet given to us by each of five women who come under these groups. We have done our best to analyse each one and give our ideas on how the diet could be improved. You may see something of yourself in one of these groups or you may find yourself in several. In any event, whichever group you are in, you should read the whole chapter and we hope our suggestions will be a help. Of course we have used fictitious names.

Group One

The first age group of women includes the teenager, the student, the bachelor girl and the young married without children. Age group 16–25 approximately.

Jane is a fairly typical example of her age group. Nineteen years old and recently married. She still lives an irregular life, rushing to work in the morning on little or no breakfast. During the day there are several appetizing snacks to relieve her fatigue and hunger. At lunch time she goes with the other girls from the office to the nearest shop to buy tempting and filling foods which are easy to eat and cheap to buy. At tea time out comes the biscuit box or someone slips out to buy cakes from that super little patisserie which has just opened up across the road. After the office there is just time to rush home, fix the false eyelashes and change before going to a

JANE

(Note: this is not a recommended diet.)

Age: 19 years
Occupation: Bank clerk
Number of children:
Ages of children:
Weight: 10 st 6 lb
Height: 5' 11"
Bone structure: Average
Under/over/average weight: Over

Day	Breakfast	Lunch	Tea	Evening meal	Snacks
Friday	Cup of coffee	2 sausage rolls Currant bun Coffee	½ sm. tin baked beans 1 fried potato	Cup of tea and wholemeal biscuits	
Saturday	Cup of coffee		Cup of tea and wholemeal biscuits		2 sm. pkts nuts Glass lemonade 6 Vodka and orange
Sunday	Cup of tea Bacon sandwich	Roast beef Brussels sprouts Cauliflower Roast potatoes			Bar of chocolate Few grapes Flake ice cream
Monday	Cup of coffee	2 hot sausage rolls. Sm. bunch grapes	1 slice bacon 1 boiled potato ½ slice bread	Cup of tea Biscuits	2 bars chocolate flake
Tuesday		2 hot sausage rolls Currant bun	Cup of tea Wholemeal biscuits	Apple turnover and custard	
Wednesday		Ham roll Pkt crisps ½ grapefruit		Cup of tea 2 slices toast Baked rice and stewed apple	Grapes
Thursday	Cup of coffee	Pkt crisps 2 rolls Orange	Boiled egg Cup of tea 2 slices toast		Bar chocolate

party or a film. Plenty of snacks there! She did, however, cook her husband an excellent Sunday lunch.

Before she was married Jane's weight was average. She was burning up many calories in anxiety over the latest love affair. Now, although she is still living a fairly exhausting life, she is more stable and contented. She will not only continue to put on weight but it is also most likely that she will be anaemic and unhealthy because her high carbohydrate diet is low in protein content and contains hardly any fresh fruit and vegetables.

Points to note. After you have filled in your diet sheet for a week you may find that you have a lot in common with Jane. It will take an effort to put yourself right but once you begin to feel fitter, and more active mentally and physically, you will find it easy to continue. You will be a girl who is fun to be with or the young wife who looks better than before she was married!

Breakfast. Make a huge effort to get up just that much earlier and have some protein and fruit before you leave the house. Although bacon and eggs are perfect, breakfast does not have to be cooked; ham and cheese are equally as good. Have a grapefruit (without sugar) or failing this an orange or apple. It *is* important to have breakfast if you go out to work. It prevents you from feeling tired and hungry early in the day; this usually results in a bun or chocolate bar at coffee time.

Lunch. If you have a proper breakfast it is possible to cut down on lunch, but this is a problem for those who eat away from home. It will make life much easier if you can enlist the cooperation of a friend who works with you. It is tempting as well as cheaper to buy rolls, sandwiches and buns from the shop next door. However, spend what you save on those fattening and unnecessary snacks. Raid your nearest delicatessen or failing this a grocer and try to concentrate on foods from our high-protein list. If working girls unite perhaps someone will produce high-protein lunches to suit them.

Tea/supper. It is just as important to eat this meal as breakfast. If you are still living at home, encourage your mother and family to join in the low carbohydrate diet.

It will do them all good. If you are cooking for yourself remember that high-protein list and plan your meals ahead. If you really are lazy it is just as easy to grill a chop as to open a tin of spaghetti. Salads need no cooking at all.

Snacks. By cutting out sweets and biscuits just think of the money you are saving.

Parties. Beware of all those little titbits. Cling to the dish which contains celery or cheese.

Group Two

Our second age group includes the mother with babies and the mother with young children. These mothers are 20 to 36 approximately.

Rachel is 29 years old with three children, and has started to go to Slimnastics classes once a week. She has never lost the weight gained during pregnancy and is increasing the excess by eating tea and finishing the children's left-overs. We are conditioned to feel guilty in this affluent society about wasting food. We feel duty bound to finish all the scraps when we think of the starving masses all over the world. This attitude of mind is understandable but will do your weight and health no good at all. The only way we can suggest to salve your conscience is for you to buy an animal or to keep hens. If you cannot keep a pet, feed the birds or the ducks on a nearby pond. Toddlers quickly grow into children and then all the food will disappear like lightning.

All mothers with young children need to do Slimnastics exercises to regain or perhaps improve their figures. Even if they are underweight they may not look it.

It can be very tiring and claustrophobic looking after small babies and toddlers. Do not neglect your own interests. Join a young wives group, play tennis and do Slimnastics with a group of friends. Make an effort to go to evening classes. Whether physically or mentally active a new interest will stimulate your mind and help to burn up those excess calories; conversely it will help put on weight by promoting relaxation if you are over-tense.

Points to note. After you have filled in your diet sheet for a week it will probably be quite obvious where you are

RACHEL

(Note: this is not a recommended diet.)

Age: 29 years
Occupation: Housewife
Number of children: 3
Ages of children: 6 yrs, 3½ yrs, 1 yr
Weight: 10 st 8 lb
Height: 5′ 6½″
Bone structure: Medium
Under/over/average weight: Over

Day	Breakfast	Lunch	Tea	Evening meal	Snacks
Friday	Boiled egg 2 Ryvita and butter Coffee	1 roll and butter Large piece cheese (about 2 oz) Coffee	2 pieces malt bread and jam 1 piece brown bread and jam	Glass of cider in evening	½ fruit yoghurt (from children's left-over lunch) Pkt crisps 2 apples
Saturday	2 scrambled eggs on toast Coffee	1 fruit yoghurt Large piece cheese Coffee and 1 biscuit	2 Scotch pancakes and jam Slice bread and jam 2 cups tea	2 kippers Bread and butter	1 apple ½ fruit yoghurt (child's left-overs) Crisps
Sunday	Boiled egg Ryvita 1 biscuit and grapefruit juice early	Roast beef Peas, beans Apple pie Cream	1 slice bread and jam Tea	Beef sandwich Drinking chocolate	2 biscuits Apple pie
Monday	Boiled egg Piece of toast	Piece of cheese		Egg and bacon and fried bread Biscuits and drinking chocolate	
Tuesday	Boiled egg 2 pieces toast	Large piece cheese Coffee	Crisps 1 crumpet and jam 2 slices bread and jam	Went out so no time for supper	
Wednesday	1 scrambled egg on toast Coffee	Very large piece cheese 2 slices of luncheon meat	2 pieces bread and jam	Liver risotto 1 apple	Large whisky
Thursday	½ slice toast Coffee	2 Ryvita and cheese Tinned pineapple and cream	2 pieces bread and butter		

going wrong. Pin the sheet up in the kitchen as a constant reminder. Have your wedding photograph near at hand together with a recent one. Do not be put off by your husband saying he likes you that way (anything for a quiet life!). He may like a dumpling now but a full-size pudding is harder to love later on.

Breakfast. It is easier to eat a properly balanced breakfast when you cook for a husband and children. Do be careful to cut out carbohydrates. If absolutely necessary allow yourself one starch-reduced roll.

Lunch. Remember that a high-protein meal is just as good for the children. Avoid the potatoes and eat fruit instead of the pudding.

Tea. Do not eat the children's tea – it is fatal. We know that cream cakes are practically irresistible. It is best not to have them in the house. Although children need some carbohydrates to give them energy they should have some protein for tea. A mother with small children is often exhausted by tea time. If you do need a pick-me-up by that time have a cup of Marmite, Bovril, or fruit juice.

Supper. A high-protein diet will suit your husband equally well. Concentrate on our high-protein list and try to present the food as attractively as possible. We feel that if you are asked out to dinner it is rude not to eat the food that has been specially prepared for you. Have a good time but cut out the roll and butter and do without the potatoes. If you feel that you have overeaten, make up for it by cutting down next day.

Group Three

This age group includes the business woman and the mother with older children. The ages are from 30 to 46 approximately.

These are your middle years. Whether you feel life is one long rush or horribly stagnant it is a time to take stock; time to reassess your looks and health so that you can meet the menopause with confidence. It is easy to think that the most exciting time has passed and that the future holds no incentive. This is far from the case and the best years can still be ahead.

Elizabeth is single, 44 years old and has reached the

top of her grade in the civil service, but feels unable to change her job. She looks after an elderly father. He does the cooking and gives her chocolates for a treat. Elizabeth feels trapped and unable to escape. The same feeling of depression and emptiness can affect a mother whose children are growing independent. They probably use her car, her daughters look glamorous and have lots of fun. She can feel unintelligent and faded.

If you feel like this you should discard your negative approach to life and acquire some positive ideas about the future. Widen your horizons, and go to evening classes. Banish the blues by making an effort to discover your hidden talent or digging up your buried ambition. It may be painting, or sailing; what about sculpture, languages, voluntary work, making wine, Cordon Bleu cookery? The possibilities are endless. Whatever your choice keep an eye on the future so that you can pursue it for many years to come.

If you feel faded give your hair a rinse, experiment with new makeup and do a Slimnastics course with a group of friends. When you are controlling your weight, eating a balanced diet and doing exercises you will have the strength and stamina to enjoy your new life. Encourage any elderly relatives who live with you to meet others of the same age. If you both have your own interests there will be so much more to share.

Even if you are active and happy, leading a busy and fulfilled life, it is easy to indulge yourself and neglect your figure and appearance. If you do not make an effort to correct your weight at this stage it will be much more difficult later.

The fourth group includes the young grandmothers and other ladies in the prime of life. Ages 40 to 60 approximately. (In the East one is said to reach one's prime in the fifties.)

Group Four

During the menopause the glands undergo a major change which can bring unpleasant physical and mental symptoms. Medical help can alleviate many of them. If you are fit and healthy, tensions and stress can be more easily managed. With patience and determination

ELIZABETH

(Note: this is not a recommended diet.)

Age: 44 years
Occupation: Economist
Number of children:
Ages of children:
Weight: 9 st 6 lb
Height: 5′ 5½″
Bone structure: Average
Under/over/average weight: Over

Day	Breakfast	Lunch	Tea	Evening meal	Snacks
Friday	Bacon and egg	Soup Fruit pie and cream		Pork chop Potatoes green beans Stewed apples cream	2 pieces chocolate
Saturday	Porridge	Bread and cheese		Sausage Mince, peas Potatoes Raspberries and cream	
Sunday	Muffin	Bacon mushrooms egg Bread		Fish, potatoes, peas Raspberries and cream	2 pieces chocolate
Monday	Muffin	Steak, mushrooms chips Roll and cheese	Bread and jam	Bread and jam	2 pieces chocolate
Tuesday	Bacon and bread	Bread and cheese		Meat pie Beans Stewed apple	Potato crisps, nuts, olives
Wednesday	Bacon and egg	Sausage roll		Pie, tomato Apples and cream	Muffin and jam Nuts
Thursday	Bacon and egg	Meat sandwich	Bread and jam	Cheese and bacon flan	

you can pass this stage with little inconvenience, emerging with renewed vigour, energy and *joie de vivre*.

Once past the menopause, the years following can be among the happiest of your life. No longer tied to the rigid timetables which children can impose, no longer forcing yourself at too fast a pace, there can now be time to relax, to talk, to study, read newspapers, form views on many subjects, enjoy the grandchildren, do the garden, make pottery, paint portraits. Without your knowing it, because you are taking a stimulating interest in everything around you, the tempo of your life is slowing down. Though mentally you are probably strenuous, physically you take a fairly leisurely pace.

Now you do not have to ferry the children around, or dash to meetings, you can leave the car behind and disdain the bus. Walk everywhere you can. It is very good exercise. Do the Slimnastics exercises too, of course. They will keep all your joints supple and help to prevent trouble in the future.

Helen is 55. She is married but has no children. She could not understand why she was consistently putting on weight although she ate no more than she did five years ago. When she was really made to consider her life at the moment she admitted that she was more contented and relaxed and less physically active than she had ever been before. Helen should have started to watch her diet as soon as she realized she was putting on weight. She must now make a real effort to cut down, as the overweight are particularly prone to the diseases of old age. She enjoys working but her job in a patisserie puts tempting delicacies within her reach.

Group Five

The fifth age group concerns the senior citizens, those of 55 and upwards.

If you are in this age group, whether you are old or not, you need plenty of rest, sleep and good food; in addition, exercise and companionship will increase your enjoyment of life. Our Slimnastics classes for senior citizens are so rewarding and such fun for everybody that we would like to encourage any clubs who do not have such classes to start our specially designed course. It has

HELEN

(Note: this is not a recommended diet.)

Age: 55 years
Occupation: Work in French patisserie
Number of children:
Ages of children:
Weight: 12 st 2 lb
Height: 5' 7½"
Bone structure: Large
Under/over/average weight: Over

Day	Breakfast	Lunch	Tea	Evening meal	Snacks
Friday	½ grapefruit Poached egg 1 slice bread Lemon tea	Ham salad 1 apple 1 cake	Tea 1 slice brown toast	Steak French salad Cheese cake Cream	Tea 2 cups coffee during day
Saturday	1 tea, 1 cup hot water and lemon 1 boiled egg 1 slice toast	Lamb chop Sprouts Bakewell tart cream	Tea 2 cups	2 eggs and chips Yoghurt Tea	Tea 1 coffee 1 cake during day
Sunday	2 rashers bacon 1 egg 1 slice brown bread ½ grapefruit	Roast beef Yorkshire pudding Cabbage ½ potato Creme caramel	Tea	Beef salad Cheese and biscuits	Coffee
Monday	Tea Boiled egg 2 slices brown bread	Cheese Tomato 2 Energen rolls 1 apple	1 hot chocolate	Cold beef and salad Yoghurt	1 coffee 1 cake during day
Tuesday	Lemon tea Poached egg 2 slices brown bread	Cheese Tomato Water biscuits Apple	Tea	Ham salad Creme caramel Tea	Coffee
Wednesday	Tea Poached egg Toast	Cheese and toast Biscuits	Tea	Cold beef and salad	Coffee
Thursday	Bacon and egg 1 slice toast, tea	Egg and chips Coffee	Tea	Vol au vent Greens	Coffee

proved very popular wherever it has been tried. At first the group tends to be small but slowly and surely the onlookers gain the courage to join in. Soon they are as enthusiastic as everyone else.

The weekly diet sheets which our women bring to their Slimnastics group are hardly a fair cross-section of this age range. Although some, like Grace, are slightly over-weight, almost without exception they all eat excellent well balanced meals. Of course it is because most of them have always taken care of their health, eaten sensibly and exercised regularly that they have avoided many of the ailments of old age and are fit and active enough to want to join our exercises. As it is they seem to get more active and energetic every week.

GRACE
(Note: this is not a recommended diet.)

Age: 68 years
Occupation: Widow living alone
Number of children: 2 sons
Ages of children:
Weight: 10 st
Height:
Bone structure: Small
Under/over/average weight: Over

Day	Breakfast	Lunch	Tea	Evening meal	Snacks
Friday	Cup of warm water Egg, bacon and tomato Cup of tea	Chicken casserole with vegetables Grapes			Cup of tea and biscuits
Saturday	Cup of warm water Buttered toast 2 cups of tea	Liver and bacon Mashed potato and tomato Apple	Poached egg on toast 2 cups of tea		Cup of tea and biscuits
Sunday	Cup of warm water Egg and bacon 2 cups of tea	Roast lamb Greens, runner beans, potato Baked apple	Slice of cake 2 cups of tea	Cup of coffee	
Monday	Cup of warm water 2 slices of buttered toast 2 cups of tea	Cold meat Greens and potatoes Apple	Tomatoes on toast 2 cups of tea		Cup of tea and biscuits
Tuesday	Cup of warm water 2 slices of buttered toast 2 Cups of Tea	Cold meat lettuce, tomatoes Apple	1 boiled egg Brown bread and butter 2 cups of tea		Cup of tea and biscuits
Wednesday	Cup of warm water Bacon and egg 2 cups of tea	Steamed fish Tomato 1 potato Apple	Scrambled egg on toast 2 cups of tea	Cup of coffee Cheese and biscuits	
Thursday	Cup of warm water 2 slices of buttered toast 2 cups of tea	Irish stew Apple	Ham and egg Roll and butter 2 cups of tea		Cup of tea and biscuits

4. Finishing Touches

If your skin is dry or caked with makeup, your poise hampered by painful feet, your bosom drooping through lack of a good bra, your hands are cracked, your hair is untidy and your clothes are crumpled, all your efforts to achieve a slim, agile and healthy body will go unnoticed. Most women are aware of the facts in this chapter, but we feel it is worth repeating them.

Do be proud of your age and enjoy it. Mutton dressed as lamb looks twice as old and becomes an object of fun. The young and mature alike have every opportunity to make the most of themselves and look really beautiful.

Health is always important. No one can have an active approach to life when dogged by ill health. Deal with any problem positively and follow the directions of your medical practitioner. However, Slimnastics will do much to improve and maintain good health. Try to get as much fresh air as possible and do not neglect other exercise. Walk everywhere you can, ignoring all forms of transport as much as this busy life will allow. Walking up stairs is one of the most energetic forms of exercise.

Sleep and relaxation are important. Sleep is the best restorer of all, recharging the batteries of young and old alike. However, it is the quality not the quantity of sleep that matters most. It is important to allow a period in which to settle down from the day's activities. To go to sleep with one's mind active will not encourage deep and refreshing rest.

One of the best ways to revive a flagging spirit is a

catnap of ten minutes during the day. The body may only relax completely for about two minutes but the rest is refreshing. If you find that you cannot sleep during the day, lie flat on your back with your legs raised above your head, your eyes closed and your muscles completely relaxed. Stay like this for ten minutes and you will be much refreshed. If you find it difficult to relax your muscles concentrate on tensing the muscles of each limb and then releasing them. Start at your toes and continue up your body to the face. By the time you have released your facial muscles you will feel totally relaxed.

Posture Equals Poise

If you have a good posture, it is easy to feel and look poised, confident and elegant. Good posture not only improves the appearance, it also aids the health of the body. It enables the respiratory, circulatory, digestive, and nervous systems to work more efficiently, giving more room for the internal organs to function correctly. Good posture allows the body to work with the minimum effort and the maximum efficiency. It also places far less strain on the muscles and joints.

What is good posture and how do you obtain it? It is the correct balance of all parts of the body, acting as one, against gravity, during any still or moving activity. Check your posture in a full-length mirror. Have you balanced all parts of the body one above the other? Now, feel tall and lift up your head and chest. Relax your shoulders and lengthen your neck. Pull in your tummy muscles, tuck your seat under and brace your thighs. While you are doing this breathe deeply and slowly.

When sitting, standing, walking, running or engaging in any other movement or position, balance all parts of your body evenly to eliminate strain.

Keep your feet and legs together when you sit or stand. When you are walking or running point your feet straight forwards, with the weight on the outside. Do not turn your feet outwards or inwards as this upsets the balance and is a strain on the nerves and circulation of the feet. Also it looks ugly!

Slimnastics exercises strengthen and tone the postural muscles so that you can maintain a balanced position.

Extra weight is posturally exhausting and puts a strain on the feet and other parts of the body.

Good posture and adequate exercise enable us to breathe more efficiently, but it is important to know the mechanics of breathing for us to use them to our best advantage.

Breathing

Inhaled air supplies oxygen to the blood, which circulates and feeds the cells, organs, glands, and nerves. Exhaled air rids the blood of waste products. The brain needs plenty of oxygen to function. Deep breathing improves metabolism, which breaks down fat and creates energy.

Open your window and take slow, deep breaths. Expand the rib cage sideways, forwards, and upwards, keeping the shoulders relaxed. The muscles which surround the rib cage are contracted, causing the air to be drawn into the lungs, and when relaxed they squeeze the air out again. Try to breathe through your nose because this warms the air and filters the dust and germs. Breathe out through the nose and the mouth. It is essential to breathe out fully. We often leave stale air at the bottom of the lungs after exhalation.

Deep breathing has a calming effect on the nerves. It can be soothing and relaxing. One can then tackle problems with renewed energy and a clearer mind.

Sparkling eyes are the gift of health and happiness. Nevertheless even healthy eyes get tired occasionally and then they should be bathed and rested under pads of damp cotton wool or lint. When you screw up your eyes against brilliant sunshine you encourage wrinkles and cause strain to the eyes themselves. Protect yourself by wearing sunglasses. If you wear ordinary glasses, make sure that the lenses are doing the job and that the frames are the most flattering for your face and personality and that they fit properly. Glasses can be a marvellous aid to beauty.

Eyes

The best protection for your teeth is regular cleaning and visits to the dentist. Make sure that there is enough calcium in your diet and avoid all sweet and sticky foods

Teeth

(but of course you will be doing this anyway). Eat plenty of raw carrots and apples and chew your food well to promote good gums.

Neck

The most important beauty aid for a lovely neck is good poise from an early age. Carry your head well and you will prevent wrinkles, double chins and a sagging jaw line. Make sure that you feed the skin of the neck as well as the face with moisturizers and skin foods. A supple skin avoids a scraggy, lined neck.

Hair

Glowing healthy hair is a shining crown. Brush regularly to stimulate the circulation of blood to the scalp and use conditioners to maintain the natural oils. Massage them in well. Older women should be extra careful not to have their hair badly or tightly permed and they should avoid having their hair completely dyed a different colour, because it is almost impossible to make up the fading skin to match and only serves to age one even more. Instead pick out the highlights and do not be afraid of going grey. Grey hair looks very attractive.

Skin

On consulting an expert on the care of skin we were surprised to learn that the young people of today have better skin and take more care of it than ever before, precisely because they start to wear makeup so much younger. They buy cleansing cream with their first lipstick as a matter of course, instead of surreptitiously patting on pancake powder and lipstick in the Ladies' Cloakroom. However healthy we may be, it is absolutely essential to feed and cleanse our skin correctly. Central heating diminishes both the natural oils and moisture in our skins and these need replacing continuously with skin foods and moisturizers. It is better to start using them early in life than to cry over dry and wrinkled skin later. Makeup acts as a protection against all the dirt in the air but do not rely on soap and water to remove it. Applying a cleansing cream with an upward movement of the hand will massage the face as well as cleanse the pores. To keep the bloom and health of the skin it is essential to include fat and vitamins in the diet and not to slim too quickly.

Bust

Basically the bust consists of a gland covered by fatty tissue and as such nothing can be done to improve its size and shape. It is possible, however, to strengthen and improve the size and shape of the muscles which are underneath the breasts and which surround and support the bust-line. These will give the bust a firmer and shapelier appearance. It is as well not to diet so drastically as to remove all the fat from the breasts; a slim figure is what we are after, not a thin beanpole. Make sure that your bra fits well and gives you the uplift you require. A little discreet padding here and there is a great idea, whatever your age, if it gives you a better outline.

Hands

You cannot expect to have good hands if you do not wear gloves to protect them when you are washing, gardening or cleaning the car. If you really find it very difficult to work in gloves remember to use a barrier cream or at least use your hand cream before you start, as this will give some protection. Make sure your diet contains enough calcium for your nails.

Legs

Smooth, shapely legs are a great asset. If your legs are not quite as shapely as you could wish, remember that darker stockings are very flattering. A suntan, true or false, will create the same illusion.

Feet

If your feet are painful it will show in your face. It is very unwise to economize on shoes. You should wear good, well-fitting shoes that are always comfortable. It is worth investing in a pair of exercise sandals which are designed to hold feet in their correct anatomical position. Regularly consult a chiropodist about any foot troubles.

Care of the Body

We 'breathe' through the pores of our skin and if they are clogged, the health will suffer. Frequent warm baths or showers will cleanse the body as well as relax the muscles. If you want to be more adventurous, a Turkish bath will make you feel really clean and a Sauna bath is most invigorating. Both will make you appear to have lost weight but it is only moisture which you will have lost in perspiration and this you will soon put back on. However, the feeling of well-being will remain. Sunbathing is a wonderful source of Vitamin D and certainly a tanned skin gives a healthy appearance. However, too much exposure to the sun will dry the skin until it becomes like leather. Make sure you keep the skin well oiled.

Makeup

You can get such excellent and up-to-the-minute advice in shops and from magazines that any detailed information here would be superfluous. With subtle use of makeup you can alter the shape of awkward features and camouflage many a blemish.

Smoking

There is no doubt about it, smoking can help you to reduce your weight. It can act as a substitute for food, and a mild stimulant. It cuts down the appetite. However, to smoke is definitely a risk to health and we would much rather encourage you to do without such artificial stimulants so that you can stay slim and beautiful for a long and healthy life.

5. Running a Slimnastics Group

To make the running of a Slimnastics group easy we thought it would be a help to give you a brief synopsis. Read through and study the whole of this chapter before filling in the charts.

When you have formed your group call them together for a preliminary discussion. For this meeting you will need a blank copy of Chart I on p. 53, and you need some scales and a tape measure. The agenda should be as follows:

(1) The place and time for the weekly meeting.

(2) Group equipment, e.g. scales, tape measure, record-player, records, chairs, toys for children (if necessary).

(3) Personal equipment – comfortable clothing and shoes, blanket, and pillow if necessary.

(4) Refreshments after Slimnastics.

(5) Fill in Chart I. This will take some time.

(6) Personal apparatus for Week I – stick and heavy sock, plastic for spot reducing (if desired).

(7) Personal apparatus to make for Week II – heavy stockings.

(8) Everyone should be asked to make an honest record of all they eat between this meeting and Week I. Follow the examples in 'The Five Ages of Women'.

(9) Check arrangements for Week I.

(10) Make a copy of Chart 4 (p. 57).

When you have filled in Chart I you should make blank copy of Chart 4 and fill this in as you progress. We have shown the different measurements in the examples.

Measure your bust, waist, hips and thigh at the beginning and end of each six weeks Slimnastics course. Remember the paragraph on spot reducing (p. 17).

Record your weight each week and at the end of the course. Then you can record the total weight and measurement loss.

Bring Chart I to each weekly meeting.

The Weekly Meeting

(1) Prepare the room or hall, e.g. remove any excess furniture, provide chairs for Groups A and B, put out toys for children if necessary, prepare refreshments.

(2) Weigh and measure those who come early, record on Chart 4.

(3) On time start the music and the exercises. Decide suitable formations for the shape of the room (p. 50).

(4) Complete the exercises for your course. The first week do Sets 7, 8 and 9 without heavy stockings.

(5) After exercises weigh and measure those who arrived late and enter in Chart 4.

(6) Have slimming refreshments.

(7) Check menus with the chapter on weight control. Decide where you went wrong and resolve to do better!

(8) Remind everyone to do their homework. These exercises (which can be found on pages 60-61 are designed so that they can be done at any time during the day either in the office, in the kitchen or in the bedroom. They are easy to remember especially if you associate each exercise with the equipment which is used. You can adapt this to the time and place; for instance, instead of the stick you can use a broom or a ruler, the weights can be replaced by a couple of tins or books, but they must of course both weigh the same. These exercises are fun to do and tone up the muscles all over the body.

(9) Help rearrange the room or hall.

Notes on the Exercises

At each meeting the group should work through a course of exercises in half an hour. Each course consists of nine or twelve sets of exercises. You should repeat each individual exercise ten times in a little less than one minute.

Each set of exercises with accompanying illustrations takes up one page of the book. At each meeting you do the course of exercises to which the charts have assigned you for six weeks. Do three exercises (on each page of your choice). Vary the choice each week, adding more if you feel so inclined. The first week do Sets 7, 8 and 9 without heavy stockings.

We have omitted the harder exercises for the two lowest courses, so as to avoid making the programme too strenuous.

The heavy stocking should not be used during the first week, and you may omit the heavy-stocking exercises that week if you wish. You will find that at the first meeting much time will be taken up by getting the group organized. Remind everyone to be prepared with the home-made equipment for the following week.

The exercises are planned so that all age groups can work together. Groups of mixed ages, such as family groups and groups at work, can be tremendous fun. For example, whatever course you are following (A, B, C, D, E or F) you will find that Set IV Exercise 2 is Side Bending (for the waistline). All ages stand with feet apart and holding a stick and do the exercise together. The difference is where the stick is held in relation to the body and how far you bend to the side.

In some cases the exercises are exactly the same, except that Course A sits on a chair to do hers, while other courses sit on the floor. The stick drawings will help to make positions and movements clear. The heavy stocking increases in weight as the courses become more advanced, but the exercises are basically the same for all age groups.

If the ages of the group are fairly close together you may all decide to follow one course. In this case still keep to the heavy stocking recommended, but it is better to be safe than sorry and you should all start on the course level of the weakest member and work up from there.

Here are some suggested formations in which the group can work for different kinds of exercises.

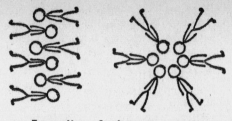

a   *Formations for leg movements – heads to the middle*

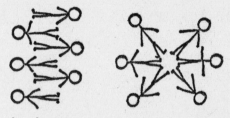

b   *Arm movements – heads away from the middle*

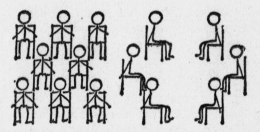

c   *Formations for chair exercises*

At the back of the book we have given a page of optional competitive exercises to be performed with a partner.

Chart Guide   You should make a blank copy of Chart I for the preliminary meeting. After you have filled in your name, address, and telephone number you will have to decide:

(1) To which *age group* you belong. It is important to read the chapter on 'The Five Ages of Women' as the ages overlap.

(2) Whether you are unfit, fairly fit or very fit.

a. You are *unfit* if you pursue a quiet occupation and do not participate in regular physical activities. (Of course, physical activity' doesn't only mean sport.)

b. You are *fairly fit* either if you have an active job or participate in a regular physical activity in or out of doors.

c. You are *very fit* if you do active work and have a regular active sporting hobby.

If you are undecided choose the *unfit* level.

(3) Now you can find from Chart 2 (page 54) the course of exercises you should follow for six weeks.

(4) Chart 2 shows you the appropriate weight of your heavy stockings.

(5) The weight of your heavy sock is also shown on Chart 2.

(6) Check your height. We have given measurements in the examples in feet and inches and metres. Measure with your back against a wall or door, no shoes, feet flat on the floor, book on your head. Ask one of the group to mark the spot and then measure.

(7) Check your bone structure. Measure your wrist; if your wrist is:

   6 in (15 cm) you are small-boned framework.
   $6\frac{1}{3}$ in (16 cm) you are average-boned framework.
   $6\frac{2}{3}$ in (17 cm) you are large-boned framework.

(8) Check the weight guide on Chart 3.
   Take 5 lb (2·5 kg) off for small bones.
   Add 5 lb (2·5 kg) for large bones.

(9) Check your present weight and enter this in Chart 1. We have shown the examples in stones and pounds and kilos. Weigh with no shoes on, dressed in light indoor clothing ready for exercises.

(10) Decide whether you are under, over or average weight, having checked the weight guide (Chart 3).

Plan a celebration at the end of your Slimnastics course. We often have a buffet supper to which all members of the group bring their own slimming speciality. Very tasty dishes can be concocted without departing from the foods which are allowed. You may have other ideas of your own – a picnic lunch or a visit to the theatre, for instance.

When you have finished your first Slimnastics course do not run away with the idea that you can just stop there. You will feel much fitter and will now have learnt to con-

Maintenance and Progression

trol your weight, but your improved health and figure will not stay that way without some effort. It is essential to maintain and continue the good work you have already started.

The six-week course will probably bring you to a natural break. Christmas, Easter and school holidays are impossible for regular meetings. It is a good idea to plan in advance to repair the damage these festivities cause. Arrange another course between the next two natural breaks. This will not only undo damage but prevent you from allowing yourself to do too much. Keep in mind that awful moment when you will once more step on those scales in front of the group. It is as well to keep a check on your weight from week to week between courses. This will encourage you to control your weight and prevent unpleasant shocks! Try and keep fit by doing your exercises regularly by yourself.

After a break you will long for the stimulus of the group again and it will be a relief to start another course. You may wish to continue with the same group or the members may all want to split up and have their own Slimnastics group. Moreover by this time, encouraged by the obvious results of your course, other friends and acquaintances will be asking to join you and the numbers may be too great for one group.

Having done regular exercises for six weeks you will now be fitter and your weight too should have changed. This will mean that you can progress to a new course. You will now have to reassess yourself and study again Chart 2 to see how you should progress, and make a new copy of Chart 1.

For the future, you should aim to maintain your health and figure by continuing your Slimnastics courses at regular intervals.

CHART 1 STATISTICS
(To be completed at the preliminary meeting)

	Jane	Rachel	Elizabeth	Helen	Grace
Address	2A The Dell	The Vicarage	Flat 3	The Bakery	The Cottage
	Broadwell	Broadwell	Eastpin	Broadpin	Henpin
Tel. No.	682	672		620	720
1 Age Group	1	2	3	4	5
2 Very fit **Fairly fit** **Unfit**	Fairly	Fairly	Fairly	Unfit	Fairly
3 Course	E	D	C	A	A
4 Heavy stocking	2 lbs	1 lb	1 lb	1 lb	$\frac{1}{2}$ lb
	1 kg	$\frac{1}{2}$ kg	$\frac{1}{2}$ kg	$\frac{1}{2}$ kg	$\frac{1}{4}$ kg
5 Heavy sock	2 lbs	1 lb	1 lb	1 lb	$\frac{1}{2}$ lb
	1 kg	$\frac{1}{2}$ kg	$\frac{1}{2}$ kg	$\frac{1}{2}$ kg	$\frac{1}{4}$ kg
6 Height	5′ 11″	5′ 6$\frac{1}{2}$″	5′ 5$\frac{1}{2}$″	5′ 7$\frac{1}{2}$″	5′ 4″
	71″	66$\frac{1}{2}$″	65$\frac{1}{2}$″	67$\frac{1}{2}$″	64″
	1·87m	1·69m	1·66m	1·77m	1·63m
7 Wrist size Large = 6$\frac{3}{4}$″ 17 cm Medium = 6$\frac{1}{4}$″ 16 cm Small = 6″ 15 cm	Medium	Medium	Medium	Large	Small
8 Ideal weight	10 st 0 lb	9 st 2 lb	9 st 2 lb	10 st 2 lb	9 st 2 lb
	140 lb	128 lb	128 lb	142 lb	128 lb
	64 kg	58 kg	58 kg	65 kg	58 kg
9 Present weight	10 st 6 lb	10 st 8 lb	9 st 6 lb	12 st 2 lb	10 st 0 lb
	146 lb	148 lb	132 lb	170 lb	140 lb
	66 kg	67 kg	60 kg	77 kg	64 kg
10 Weight average **over/under**	Over	Over	Average	Over	Over

CHART 2

	1	2	3	4	5
Five Ages of Women See Chapter 3	16–25 yrs	20–36 yrs	30–46 yrs	40–60 yrs	55 upwards
Courses of Exercises					
½ hour — Unfit	D	C	B	A	A
Once a — Fairly fit	E	D	C	B	A
week — Very fit	F	E	D	C	B
Two Heavy Stockings For arms or legs	2–4 lb 1–2 kg	1–3 lb ½–1½ kg	1–3 lb ½–1½ kg	1–2 lb ½–1 kg	½–1 lb ¼–½ kg
One Heavy Sock For holding in hands and feet.	2 lb 1 kg	1 lb ½ kg	1 lb ½ kg	1 lb ½ kg	½ lb ¼ kg

CHART 3 IDEAL WEIGHT GUIDE

Height	15–25 yrs	25–35 yrs	35–45 yrs	45 years and over
4′ 10″ 58″ 1·47m	7 st 5 lb 103 lb 47·5 kg	7 st 8 lb 106 lb 48 kg	7 st 11 lb 109 lb 49·5 kg	8 st 112 lb 51 kg
4′ 11″ 59″ 1·49m	7 st 8 lb 106 lb 48 kg	7 st 11 lb 109 lb 49·5 kg	8 st 112 lb 51 kg	8 st 2 lb 114 lb 52 kg
5′ 0″ 60″ 1·52m	7 st 11 lb 109 lb 49·5 kg	8 st 112 lb 51 kg	8 st 2 lb 114 lb 52 kg	8 st 5 lb 117 lb 53 kg
5′ 1″ 61″ 1·55m	8 st 112 lb 51 kg	8 st 2 lb 114 lb 52 kg	8 st 5 lb 117 lb 53 kg	8 st 8 lb 120 lb 54·5 kg
5′ 2″ 62″ 1·57m	8 st 2 lb 114 lb 52 kg	8 st 5 lb 117 lb 53 kg	8 st 8 lb 120 lb 54·5 kg	8 st 11 lb 123 lb 56 kg
5′ 3″ 63″ 1·6m	8 st 5 lb 117 lb 53·6 kg	8 st 8 lb 120 lb 54·5 kg	8 st 11 lb 123 lb 56 kg	9 st 126 lb 57 kg
5′ 4″ 64″ 1·62	8 st 8 lb 120 lb 54·5 kg	8 st 11 lb 123 lb 56 kg	9 st 126 lb 57 kg	9 st 2 lb 128 lb 58 kg
5′ 5″ 65″ 1·65m	8 st 11 lb 123 lb 56 kg	9 st 126 lb 57 kg	9 st 2 lb 128 lb 58 kg	9 st 5 lb 131 lb 59·5 kg
5′ 6″ 66″ 1·68m	9 st 126 lb 57 kg	9 st 2 lb 128 lb 59·5 kg	9 st 5 lb 131 lb 59·5 kg	9 st 8 lb 134 lb 61 kg
5′ 7″ 67″ 1·7m	9 st 2 lb 128 lb 58 kg	9 st 5 lb 131 lb 59·5 kg	9 st 8 lb 134 lb 61 kg	9 st 11 lb 137 lb 62 kg
5′ 8″ 68″ 1·73m	9 st 5 lb 131 lb 59·5 kg	9 st 8 lb 134 lb 61 kg	9 st 11 lb 137 lb 62 kg	10 st 140 lb 63·5 kg
5′ 9″ 69″ 1·75m	9 st 8 lb 134 lb 61 kg	9 st 11 lb 137 lb 62 kg	10 st 140 lb 63·5 kg	10 st 2 lb 142 lb 64·5 kg
5′ 10″ 70″ 1·78m	9 st 11 lb 137 lb 62·6 kg	10 st 140 lb 63·5 kg	10 st 2 lb 142 lb 64·5 kg	10 st 5 lb 145 lb 66 kg

Height	15–25 yrs	25–35 yrs	35–45 yrs	45 years and over
5′ 11″	10 st	10 st 2 lb	10 st 5 lb	10 st 8 lb
71″	140 lb	142 lb	145 lb	148 lb
1·80m	63·5 kg	64·5 kg	66 kg	67 kg
6′ 0″	10 st 2 lb	10 st 5 lb	10 st 8 lb	10 st 11 lb
72″	142 lb	145 lb	148 lb	151 lb
1·83m	64·5 kg	66·5 kg	68 kg	69·5 kg

Take 5lbs (2.5kg) off for small bones.
Add 5lbs (2.5kg) for large bones. See p. 53 (7).

You are overweight if you are more than 7lbs (3.5kg) over your ideal weight.

You are underweight If you are more than 7lbs (3.5kg) under your ideal weight.

CHART 4 PROGRESS
(To be made out blank and filled in weekly)

Measurements	Jane in	cm	Rachel in	cm	Elizabeth in	cm	Helen in	cm	Grace in	cm
Week 1										
Bust	35	89	36	91·5	35	89	40	101·5	34	86
Waist	28	71	28	71	25	63·5	32	81	26	66
Hips	38	96·5	39	99	37	94	44	111·5	36	91·5
Thigh	23	58·5	22½	57	22	56	25	63·5	21	53·5
Measurements Week 6										
Bust	35	89	35	89	34	86	38	96·5	34	86
Waist	27	68·5	26	66	25	63·5	30	76	25	63·5
Hips	34	86	37	94	35	89	40	101·5	35	89
Thigh	22	56	22	56	22	56	24	61	20	51

Body weight	Jane	Rachel	Elizabeth	Helen	Grace
Week 1	10 st 6 lb / 146 lb / 66 kg	10 st 8 lb / 148 lb / 67 kg	9 st 10 lb / 136 lb / 62 kg	12 st 2 lb / 170 lb / 77 kg	10 st / 140 lb / 64 kg
Week 2	10 st 6 lb / 146 lb / 66 kg	10 st 6 lb / 146 lb / 66 kg	9 st 8 lb / 134 lb / 61 kg	12 st / 168 lb / 76 kg	9 st 12 lb / 138 lb / 62·5 kg
Week 3	10 st 4 lb / 144 lb / 65·5 kg	10 st 4 lb / 144 lb / 65·5 kg	9 st 5 lb / 131 lb / 59·5 kg	12 st 1 lb / 169 lb / 76·5 kg	9 st 10 lb / 136 lb / 62 kg
Week 4	10 st 3 lb / 143 lb / 65 kg	10 st / 140 lb / 63·5 kg	9 st 3 lb / 129 lb / 58·5 kg	11 st 10 lb / 164 lb / 74·5 kg	9 st 13 lb / 139 lb / 63 kg
Week 5	10 st 3 lb / 143 lb / 65 kg	9 st 12 lb / 138 lb / 62·5 kg	9 st 4 lb / 130 lb / 59 kg	11 st 5 lb / 159 lb / 72 kg	9 st 6 lb / 132 lb / 60 kg
Week 6	10 st / 140 lb / 63·5 kg	9 st 12 lb / 138 lb / 62·5 kg	9 st 2 lb / 128 lb / 58 kg	11 st 2 lb / 156 lb / 71 kg	9 st 6 lb / 132 lb / 60 kg
Weight loss	6 lb / 2·5 kg	10 lb / 4·5 kg	8 lb / 4 kg	14 lb / 6 kg	8 lb / 4 kg
Measurement loss	6" / 15 cm	5½" / 14 cm	3" / 8 cm	9" / 23 cm	3" / 8 cm

6. The Exercises

DAILY EXERCISES SET I To be done every day at home or at work

Name	Starting Position	Movement	Poise	To Improve
1. Head circling	Sitting on chair. Feet on floor	Head circling slowly. Change direction	Sit tall	Neck
2. Knees lift	Sitting in chair knees bent. Legs together. Hold back of chair	Drop head on chest. Lift knees. Point toes. Lower	As for Exercise 1	Tummy
3. Knees bend and stretch	Standing heels together gripping chair or table	Up on toes, slowly bend both knees out sideways. Go right down and up	Straight back	Hips, legs, ankles
4. Leg lift backwards	As for Exercise 3	Up on toes, stretch one leg behind and arch back. Repeat other leg	Stand tall, straight back	Hips, thighs
5. Side bending	Standing feet apart holding stick at each end above head	Bend to alternate sides, shoulders facing front	Stand tall, feet facing front. Head up	Waist
6. Bust level stick rotation	Standing feet apart holding stick at each end	Stick at bust level twist side to side, looking backwards each time	As for Exercise 5	Shoulders, waist, hips

DAILY EXERCISES SET II   To be done every day at home or at work

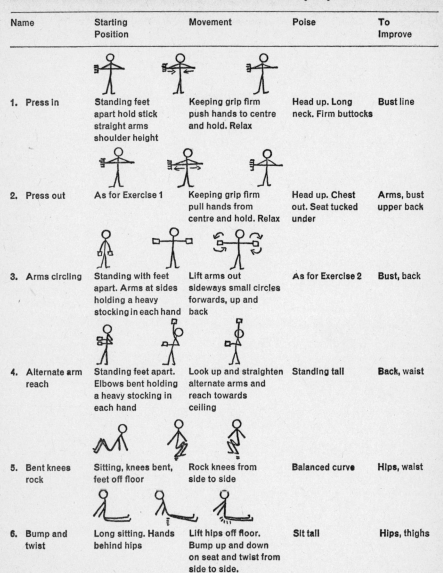

Name	Starting Position	Movement	Poise	To Improve
1. Press in	Standing feet apart hold stick straight arms shoulder height	Keeping grip firm push hands to centre and hold. Relax	Head up. Long neck. Firm buttocks	Bust line
2. Press out	As for Exercise 1	Keeping grip firm pull hands from centre and hold. Relax	Head up. Chest out. Seat tucked under	Arms, bust upper back
3. Arms circling	Standing with feet apart. Arms at sides holding a heavy stocking in each hand	Lift arms out sideways small circles forwards, up and back	As for Exercise 2	Bust, back
4. Alternate arm reach	Standing feet apart. Elbows bent holding a heavy stocking in each hand	Look up and straighten alternate arms and reach towards ceiling	Standing tall	Back, waist
5. Bent knees rock	Sitting, knees bent, feet off floor	Rock knees from side to side	Balanced curve	Hips, waist
6. Bump and twist	Long sitting. Hands behind hips	Lift hips off floor. Bump up and down on seat and twist from side to side.	Sit tall	Hips, thighs

COURSE A SET I Warm-up exercises

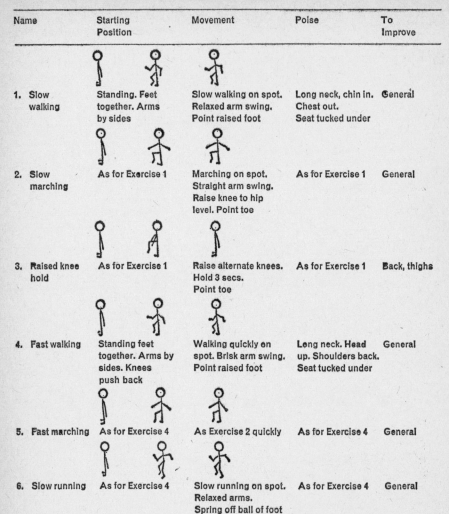

Name	Starting Position	Movement	Poise	To Improve
1. Slow walking	Standing. Feet together. Arms by sides	Slow walking on spot. Relaxed arm swing. Point raised foot	Long neck, chin in. Chest out. Seat tucked under	General
2. Slow marching	As for Exercise 1	Marching on spot. Straight arm swing. Raise knee to hip level. Point toe	As for Exercise 1	General
3. Raised knee hold	As for Exercise 1	Raise alternate knees. Hold 3 secs. Point toe	As for Exercise 1	Back, thighs
4. Fast walking	Standing feet together. Arms by sides. Knees push back	Walking quickly on spot. Brisk arm swing. Point raised foot	Long neck. Head up. Shoulders back. Seat tucked under	General
5. Fast marching	As for Exercise 4	As Exercise 2 quickly	As for Exercise 4	General
6. Slow running	As for Exercise 4	Slow running on spot. Relaxed arms. Spring off ball of foot	As for Exercise 4	General

COURSE A SET II Chair exercises – sitting

Name	Starting Position	Movement	Poise	To Improve
1. One knee raise	Sitting. Feet together. Holding chair seat	Lift alternate knees. Point toe	Head up. Long neck. Shoulders back	Waist, hips, legs
2. Hips raise	Sitting on edge of chair. Hold chair seat. Legs straight in front	Lift hips off chair. Weight on arms	Straight back. Shoulders down	Back, hips
3. Leg crossover	As for Exercise 1. Bent legs	Cross bent right leg over left and lean to left. Repeat alternate legs	As for Exercise 2	Waist, hips
4. Touch toes upward stretch	Sitting feet together	Touch toes. Head on knees. Stretch tall. Arms above head. Look at fingers	Long neck	Back, waist, hips
5. Both knees raise	Sitting. Legs together. Hold back of chair	Raise both knees together. Point toes	Sit tall. Long neck	Waist, thighs
6. Waist twist	Sitting. Feet together	Twist arms and knees in opposite directions	Long back. Head up and face front	Waist

COURSE A SET III Chair exercises – standing

Name	Starting Position	Movement	Poise	To Improve
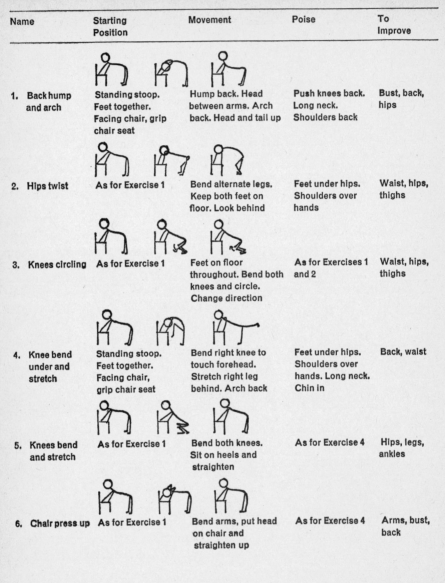
1. Back hump and arch	Standing stoop. Feet together. Facing chair, grip chair seat	Hump back. Head between arms. Arch back. Head and tail up	Push knees back. Long neck. Shoulders back	Bust, back, hips
2. Hips twist	As for Exercise 1	Bend alternate legs. Keep both feet on floor. Look behind	Feet under hips. Shoulders over hands	Waist, hips, thighs
3. Knees circling	As for Exercise 1	Feet on floor throughout. Bend both knees and circle. Change direction	As for Exercises 1 and 2	Waist, hips, thighs
4. Knee bend under and stretch	Standing stoop. Feet together. Facing chair, grip chair seat	Bend right knee to touch forehead. Stretch right leg behind. Arch back	Feet under hips. Shoulders over hands. Long neck. Chin in	Back, waist
5. Knees bend and stretch	As for Exercise 1	Bend both knees. Sit on heels and straighten	As for Exercise 4	Hips, legs, ankles
6. Chair press up	As for Exercise 1	Bend arms, put head on chair and straighten up	As for Exercise 4	Arms, bust, back

COURSE A SET IV Standing exercises with stick

Name	Starting Position	Movement	Poise	To Improve
1. Hip level stick rotation	Standing feet apart holding stick at each end	Keeping stick at hip level twist side to side looking backwards	Standing tall. Long neck. Head up, chin in. Face front	Back, waist, hips
2. Side	As for Exercise 1 Holding stick behind hips	Bend to alternate sides. Shoulders face front	As for Exercise 1	Waist
3. Stretch up touch toes	As for Exercise 1. Holding stick in front of hips	Straight arm stretch above head, bend down touch toes. Eyes on stick	As for Exercise 1	Back, waist, hips
4. Half circle swing	Stoop. Standing legs apart. Arms hang down holding stick	Relaxed knees. Swing stick upwards from side to side. Keep head central	Long neck. Relaxed shoulders	Back, bust, waist
5. Arm marching with partners	Stand facing partner. Arms by sides, holding sticks	Swing arms forwards and backwards. Turn body each time	Stand tall. Long neck. Shoulders back	Shoulders, waist, hips
6. Arms raise and lower facing partner	As for Exercise 5	Both arms sideways raise, stretch above head and lower	As for Exercise 5	Arms, bust

COURSE A SET V   Exercises with partner, using heavy sock

Name	Starting Position	Movement	Poise	To Improve
1. Throw and catch	Standing at a distance facing partner	Throw and catch sock with partner. Step forward with opposite foot to arm	Tall, balanced	All parts
2. Turn pass	Standing back to back. Feet apart	Both turn to right. Pass sock with two hands. Repeat other side	Feet still, facing front. Arms straight	Back, waist
3. Pass over and under	As for Exercise 2	Pass sock over head and between legs. Sock in both hands and watch throughout	Balanced and graceful. Arms straight	Back, hips
4. Foot throw	Standing facing partner. Sock on one foot	Lift foot and throw sock to partner who catches it and puts it on her own foot	Keep tall and balanced	Hips, thighs
5. Throw between legs	Standing at a distance one behind the other. Feet apart	Partner with sock bends and throws it between legs for partner to catch	Relaxed and balanced	Back, hips
6. Throw over head	As for Exercise 5	Partner with sock stretches up, and throws sock over head to partner behind	As for Exercise 4	Back, hips

COURSE A SET VI Exercises for extremities – sitting in chair

Name	Starting Position	Movement	Poise	To Improve
1. Foot circling	Sitting in chair. Legs straight. Toes pointed	Toes up, out and down. Circle feet	Sit tall	Feet, ankles, calves
2. Head circling	Sitting in chair. Feet on floor	Head circling slowly. Change direction	As for Exercise 1	Neck
3. Wrist circling. Stretch finger	As for Exercise 2	Elbows bent touching sides. Circle wrist. Clench fists and stretch fingers 10 times	As for Exercise 1	Hands, wrist, forearm
4. Faces	Sitting in chair, Feet on floor	With eyes and mouth exaggerate E E, O O, then squeeze face, relax, smile. Repeat	Sit tall	Facial and chin muscles
5. Shoulder roll	As for Exercise 4	Lift shoulders to ears and circle up, back and down 10 times	As for Exercise 4	Neck, shoulders, bust
6. Banging	As for Exercise 4	With clenched fist bang tummy, thighs, hips. Stop, relax, breathe deeply. Repeat	As for Exercise 4	Increasing circulation, and disperse the fat

COURSE A SET VII Chair exercises with heavy stockings

Name	Starting Position	Movement	Poise	To Improve
1. Cross over chest	Sitting in chair. Feet together. Hold heavy stocking in each hand	Cross arms in front of chest and down by sides	Sit tall	Shoulders, bust, back
2. Alternate fist push	As for Exercise 1	Raise alternate arms and push forwards	As for Exercise 1	Bust, back
3. Raise arms forwards, out and down	As for Exercise 1	Raise both arms forwards and up to shoulder level, sideways and lower	Sit tall. Arms straight	Shoulders, bust, back
4. Alternate arm stretch up	Sitting in chair. Feet together. Hold heavy stocking in each hand	Raise one arm up over head and lower and at same time lift other arm	Sit tall. Arms straight	Shoulders, bust, back, waist
5. Lift arms behind and front	As for Exercise 4	Lean forwards and lift straight arms backwards. Sit up and swing arms forwards	As for Exercise 4	Shoulders, bust, back, hips
6. Lift arms sideways up and down	As for Exercise 4	Lift both arms sideways above head. Slowly down sideways	As for Exercise 4	Trunk, arms

COURSE A SET VIII
Leg exercises with heavy stockings, using chair

Name	Starting Position	Movement	Poise	To Improve
1. One knee raise	Sitting on chair Stocking tied round ankles and ball of foot	Holding seat of chair, lift right knee and lower slowly. Repeat alternate knees	Sit tall. Shoulders back. Tummy in	Waist, thighs
2. Straight leg cross over	As for Exercise 1	Lift right foot and straighten leg. Cross over left knee. Lean to left. Repeat with right leg	As for Exercise 1	Waist, hips, thighs
3. Leg lift sideways	Standing sideways on to chair back. Hold with one hand	Lift leg sideways and down. Point toe. Turn and repeat other leg	Stand tall	Waist, hips, thighs
4. Leg lift backwards	Standing facing chair back. Two hands support	Lift one leg backwards and lower. Repeat other leg	Stand tall with straight back	Hips, thighs
5. Leg circling sideways	Standing sideways to chair. Hold with one hand	Lift one leg sideways and circle. Turn and repeat other side	As for Exercise 4	Waist, hips, thighs
6. Knees lift	Sitting on chair. Knees bent. Legs together. Hold back of chair	Lift knees. Point toes. Lower	Sit tall	Thighs, waist

COURSE A SET IX Arm exercises with heavy stockings

Name	Starting Position	Movement	Poise	To Improve
1. Arms circling	Standing with feet apart. Arms at sides. Heavy stockings held in hands	Lift arms out sideways. Circle forwards, up and back	Stand tall. Long neck. Seat tucked under	Bust, back
2. Shoulders lift up and down	As for Exercise 1	Lift shoulders up to ears and lower	As for Exercise 1	Shoulders
3. Arms crossed and stretched sideways	Stoop standing. Arms hanging down	Cross arms and fling open sideways. Repeat	Straight spine. Long neck	Back
4. Alternate arm reach high	Standing feet apart. Elbows bent	Look up and straighten alternate arms and reach towards ceiling	Standing tall	Back, waist
5. Arms raise sideways	Standing feet apart. Arms by sides	Lift both arms out sideways above head. Lower out sideways and down	As for Exercise 4	Trunk
6. Alternate arm reach forward	As for Exercise 4	Reach forwards straightening alternate arms	As for Exercise 4	Bust, back

COURSE B SET I Warm-up exercises

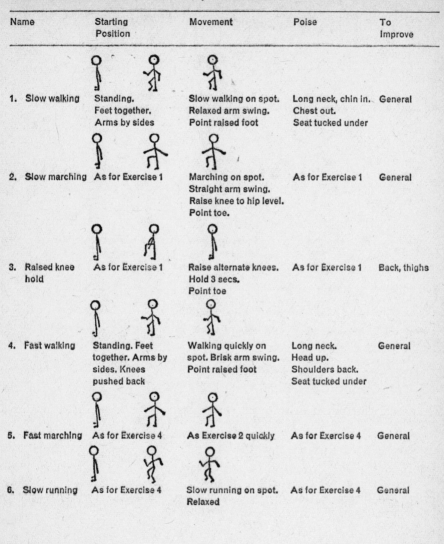

Name	Starting Position	Movement	Poise	To Improve
1. Slow walking	Standing. Feet together. Arms by sides	Slow walking on spot. Relaxed arm swing. Point raised foot	Long neck, chin in. Chest out. Seat tucked under	General
2. Slow marching	As for Exercise 1	Marching on spot. Straight arm swing. Raise knee to hip level. Point toe.	As for Exercise 1	General
3. Raised knee hold	As for Exercise 1	Raise alternate knees. Hold 3 secs. Point toe	As for Exercise 1	Back, thighs
4. Fast walking	Standing. Feet together. Arms by sides. Knees pushed back	Walking quickly on spot. Brisk arm swing. Point raised foot	Long neck. Head up. Shoulders back. Seat tucked under	General
5. Fast marching	As for Exercise 4	As Exercise 2 quickly	As for Exercise 4	General
6. Slow running	As for Exercise 4	Slow running on spot. Relaxed	As for Exercise 4	General

COURSE B SET II Floor exercises – sitting

Name	Starting Position	Movement	Poise	To Improve
1. One-knee raise	Long sitting. Hands on floor behind hips. Point toes	Bend alternate knees. Put right toe on top of left knee cap	Sit tall. Tummy in	Waist
2. Hips raise	As for Exercise 1	Lift hips off floor. Hold and lower	As for Exercise 1	Back, waist, hips
3. Leg crossover	As for Exercise 1	Cross right leg over left. Lean to left. Shoulders front. Alternate legs	As for Exercise 1	Waist, hips, thighs
4. Back curl and arch	Sitting. Knees bent. Hands on floor behind hips	Head on knees. Arms embrace legs. Arms back. Look up at ceiling	Head up. Shoulders down. Long neck	Back, waist, hips
5. Both knees raise	Long sitting	Raise both legs, bend knees and put feet on floor. Return	Sit tall	Waist, thighs hips
6. Seat walking	Long sitting, arms bent	Progress along floor on seat with bent arms used as in running	Sit tall	Back, waist, hips

COURSE B SET III Chair exercises – standing

Name	Starting Position	Movement	Poise	To Improve
1. Back hump and arch	Standing stoop. Feet together. Facing chair, grip chair seat	Hump back. Head between arms. Arch back. Head and tail up	Push knees back. Long neck. Shoulders back	Bust, back, hips
2. Hips twist	As for Exercise 1	Bend right leg, twist hips to right. Keep both feet on floor. Look to right	Feet under hips. Shoulders over hands	Waist, hips, thighs
3. Knees circling	As for Exercise 1	Feet on floor throughout. Bend both knees and circle. Change direction	As for Exercises 1 and 2	Waist, hips, thighs
4. Knee bend under and stretch	Standing stoop. Feet together. Facing chair, grip chair seat	Bend right knee to touch forehead. Stretch right leg behind. Arch back	Feet under hips. Shoulders over hands. Long neck. Chin in	Back, waist
5. Knees bend and stretch	As for Exercise 1	Bend both knees. Sit on heels and straighten	As for Exercise 4	Hips, legs, ankles
6. Chair press up	As for Exercise 1	Bend arms, put head on chair and straighten up	As for Exercise 4	Arms, bust, back

COURSE B SET IV Standing exercises with stick

Name	Starting Position	Movement	Poise	To Improve
1. Waist-level stick rotation	Standing feet apart holding stick at each end	Stick at waist level, twist side to side looking backwards each time	Stand tall. Long neck. Head up, chin in. Face front	Back, arms, waist, hips
2. Side bending	As for Exercise 1, holding stick between elbows behind waist	Bend to alternate sides, shoulders face front	As for Exercise 1	Waist
3. Stretch up behind head, touch toes	As for Exercise 1, with stick in front of hips	Stretch stick above head, bend arms and place behind neck. Stretch up, touch toes	As for Exercise 1	Shoulders, waist, hips
4. Half circle swing	Stoop, standing straight, legs apart. Arms hang down. Hands holding stick	Relaxed knees. Swing stick upwards from side to side, keep head central	Long neck. Relaxed shoulders	Back, bust, waist
5. Bending facing partner	Long sitting, facing partner, legs apart, holding sticks	Pull and push sticks backwards and forwards with partner	Straight back, shoulders down	Back, bust, waist
6. Side rock facing partner	As for Exercise 5	Bend to alternate sides following partner	As for Exercise 5	Shoulders, bust, waist, hips

COURSE B SET V Exercises with partner, using heavy sock

Name	Starting Position	Movement	Poise	To Improve
		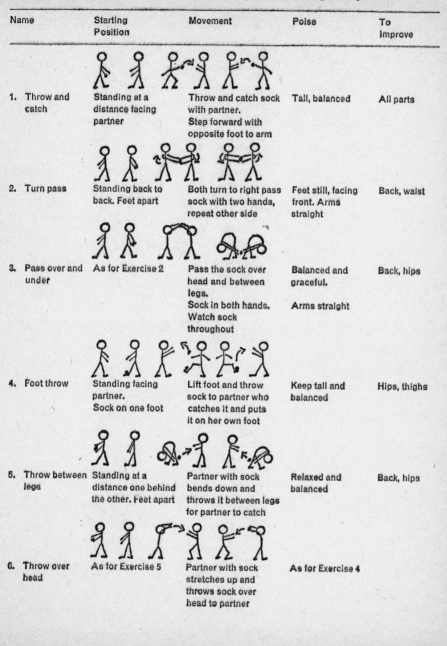		
1. Throw and catch	Standing at a distance facing partner	Throw and catch sock with partner. Step forward with opposite foot to arm	Tall, balanced	All parts
2. Turn pass	Standing back to back. Feet apart	Both turn to right pass sock with two hands, repeat other side	Feet still, facing front. Arms straight	Back, waist
3. Pass over and under	As for Exercise 2	Pass the sock over head and between legs. Sock in both hands. Watch sock throughout	Balanced and graceful. Arms straight	Back, hips
4. Foot throw	Standing facing partner. Sock on one foot	Lift foot and throw sock to partner who catches it and puts it on her own foot	Keep tall and balanced	Hips, thighs
5. Throw between legs	Standing at a distance one behind the other. Feet apart	Partner with sock bends down and throws it between legs for partner to catch	Relaxed and balanced	Back, hips
6. Throw over head	As for Exercise 5	Partner with sock stretches up and throws sock over head to partner	As for Exercise 4	

COURSE B SET VI Exercises for extremities – long sitting

Name	Starting Position	Movement	Poise	To Improve
1. Foot circling	Long sitting	Toes up, out and down. Circle feet	Sit tall	Feet, ankles, calves
2. Head circling	As for Exercise 1	Head circling slowly. Change direction	As for Exercise 1	Neck
3. Wrist circling. Stretch fingers	As for Exercise 1	Elbows bent but touching sides. Circle wrist (10). Clench fists and stretch fingers (10).	As for Exercise 1	Hand, wrists, forearm
4. Faces	Long sitting	With eyes and mouth exaggerate E E, O O, then squeeze face, relax, smile. Repeat	Sit tall	Facial and chin muscles
5. Shoulder roll	As for Exercise 4	Lift shoulders to ears and circle up, back and down 10 times	As for Exercise 4	Neck, shoulders, bust
6. Banging	As for Exercise 4	With clenched fist bang tummy, thighs, hips. Stop, relax, breathe deeply. Repeat	As for Exercise 4	Increasing circulation and disperse the fat

COURSE B SET VII Exercises with heavy stockings

Name	Starting Position	Movement	Poise	To Improve
1. Cross over chest	Sitting in chair. Feet together. Hold heavy stocking in each hand	Cross arms in front of chest and down by sides	Sit tall	Bust, back
2. Alternate fist push	As for Exercise 1	Raise alternate arms and push forwards	As for Exercise 1	Bust, back
3. Raise arms forwards, out and down	As for Exercise 1	Raise both arms forwards and up to shoulder level, sideways and lower	Sit tall. Arms straight	Bust, back
4. Alternate arm stretch up	Sitting in chair. Feet together. Hold heavy stocking in each hand	Raise one arm up over head and lower and at same time lift other arm	Sit tall. Arms straight	Bust, back, waist
5. Lift arms behind and front	As for Exercise 4	Lean forwards and lift straight arms backwards . Sit up and swing arms forwards	As for Exercise 4	Bust, back, hips
6. Lift arms sideways up and down	As for Exercise 4	Lift both arms sideways above head. Slowly down sideways	As for Exercise 4	Trunk, arms

COURSE B SET VIII Leg exercises with heavy stockings, using chair

Name	Starting Position	Movement	Poise	To Improve
1. One knee raise	Sitting on chair. Stockings tied round ankles and ball of foot	Holding seat of chair, lift right knee and lower slowly. Repeat alternate knees	Sit tall. Shoulders back. Tummy in	Tummy, thighs
2. Straight leg Cross	As for Exercise 1	Lift right foot and straighten leg. Cross over left knee. Lean to left. Repeat with right leg	As for Exercise 1	Waist, hips, thighs
3. Leg lift sideways	Standing sideways on to chair back. Hold with one hand	Lift leg sideways and down. Point toe. Turn and repeat other leg	Stand tall	Waist, hips, thighs
4. Leg lift backwards	Standing facing chair back. Two hands support	Lift one leg backwards and lower. Repeat other leg	Stand tall with straight back	Hips, thighs
5. Leg circling sideways	Standing sideways to chair. Hold with one hand	Lift one leg sideways and circle. Turn and repeat other side	As for Exercise 4	Waist, hips, thighs
6. Knees lift	Sitting on chair. knees bent. Legs together. Hold seat of chair	Raise knees. Point toes. Lower	Sit tall	Thighs, waist

COURSE B SET IX   Arm exercises with heavy stockings

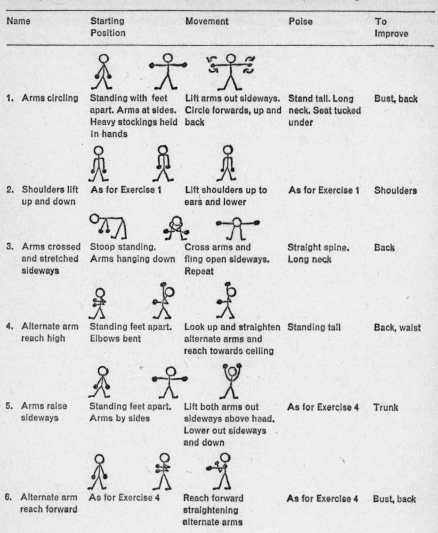

Name	Starting Position	Movement	Poise	To Improve
1. Arms circling	Standing with feet apart. Arms at sides. Heavy stockings held in hands	Lift arms out sideways. Circle forwards, up and back	Stand tall. Long neck. Seat tucked under	Bust, back
2. Shoulders lift up and down	As for Exercise 1	Lift shoulders up to ears and lower	As for Exercise 1	Shoulders
3. Arms crossed and stretched sideways	Stoop standing. Arms hanging down	Cross arms and fling open sideways. Repeat	Straight spine. Long neck	Back
4. Alternate arm reach high	Standing feet apart. Elbows bent	Look up and straighten alternate arms and reach towards ceiling	Standing tall	Back, waist
5. Arms raise sideways	Standing feet apart. Arms by sides	Lift both arms out sideways above head. Lower out sideways and down	As for Exercise 4	Trunk
6. Alternate arm reach forward	As for Exercise 4	Reach forward straightening alternate arms	As for Exercise 4	Bust, back

COURSE C SET I Warm-up exercises

Name	Starting Position	Movement	Poise	To Improve
1. Walking	Standing. Feet together. Arms by sides	Slow walking on spot. Relaxed arm swing. Point raised foot	Head up. Long neck. Chin in. Chest out. Seat tucked under	General
2. Marching	As for Exercise 1	Marching on spot. Straight arm swing. Raise knee to hip level. Point toe	As for Exercise 1	General
3. High knee hold	As for Exercise 1	Raise alternate knees to chest level. Hold 3 secs. Point toe	As for Exercise 1	Back thighs, legs
4. Running	Standing. Feet together. Arms by sides	Running on spot. Relaxed arms. Spring off ball of foot. Point toe	Long neck. Head up. Shoulders back. Seat tucked under	General
5. Running knees up	As for Exercise 4	Running on spot. Lift knee to hip level	As for Exercise 4	General
6. High knee running	As for Exercise 4	As for Exercise 5 with knees raised to waist level	As for Exercise 4	General

COURSE C SET II Floor exercises – sitting

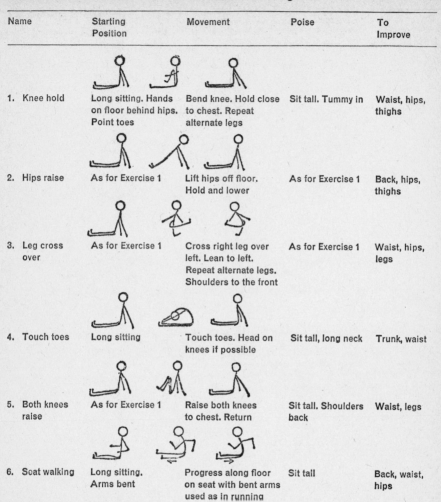

Name	Starting Position	Movement	Poise	To Improve
1. Knee hold	Long sitting. Hands on floor behind hips. Point toes	Bend knee. Hold close to chest. Repeat alternate legs	Sit tall. Tummy in	Waist, hips, thighs
2. Hips raise	As for Exercise 1	Lift hips off floor. Hold and lower	As for Exercise 1	Back, hips, thighs
3. Leg cross over	As for Exercise 1	Cross right leg over left. Lean to left. Repeat alternate legs. Shoulders to the front	As for Exercise 1	Waist, hips, legs
4. Touch toes	Long sitting	Touch toes. Head on knees if possible	Sit tall, long neck	Trunk, waist
5. Both knees raise	As for Exercise 1	Raise both knees to chest. Return	Sit tall. Shoulders back	Waist, legs
6. Seat walking	Long sitting. Arms bent	Progress along floor on seat with bent arms used as in running	Sit tall	Back, waist, hips

R–S–F

COURSE C SET III Floor exercises – hands and knees

Name	Starting Position	Movement	Poise	To Improve
1. Back hump and arch	On hands and knees. Hands under shoulders, knees under hips	Hump back. Head between arms. Tuck seat under. Arch back	Head up. Chin in. Long neck. Seat tucked under	Bust, waist, hips
2. Hip twist	As for Exercise 1	Twist hips to right. Turn head and look at right hip. Repeat other side	As for Exercise 1	Waist, hips
3. Waist circling	As for Exercise 1	Hump back, side, arch back, other side. Change direction	As for Exercise 1	Waist, hips
4. Knee bend under and stretch	On hands and knees. Hands under shoulders, knees under hips	Bend right knee to touch forehead. Right leg behind. Arch back	Head up. Chin in. Long neck. Seat tucked under	Waist, hips
5. Press forwards and rock backwards	As for Exercise 1	Lie flat by moving body forwards. Back to start. Sit on heels, head on floor	As for Exercise 4	General
6. Hip high and lower	As for Exercise 1 but toes tucked under	Raise hips, straight legs. Lower hips, hands and feet still. Head up	As for Exercise 1	Waist, hips, legs

COURSE C SET IV Standing exercises with stick

Name	Starting Position	Movement	Poise	To Improve
Bust level stick rotation	Standing feet apart holding stick at each end	Stick at bust level twist side to side, looking backwards each time	Stand tall. Feet facing front. Long neck, head up	Shoulders, waist, hips
2. Side bending	As for Exercise 1 holding stick behind neck	Bend to alternate sides, shoulders face front	As for Exercise 1	Waist
3. Stretch stick behind, touch toes	As for Exercise 1 holding stick in front of hips	Stretch, stick above head, bend arms and place behind shoulders. Stretch up, touch toes	As for Exercise 1	Back, bust, hips
4. Half circle swing	Stoop, standing legs apart. Arms hang down. Hands holding stick	Relaxed knees. Swing stick upwards from side to side, keep head central	Long neck. Relaxed shoulders	Back, bust, waist
5. Bending facing partner	Long sitting, facing partner, legs apart. Holding stick between you	Pull and push sticks backwards and forwards with partner	Straight back shoulders down	Back, bust, waist
6. Side rock facing partner	As for Exercise 5	Bend to alternate sides following partner	As for Exercise 5	Shoulders, bust, waist hips

COURSE C SET V Exercises with partner, using heavy sock

Name	Starting Position	Movement	Poise	To Improve
1. Under leg throw	Standing at a distance facing partner	Lift one leg and throw sock to partner under leg. Use alternate legs	Balanced and tall	Waist, hips, thighs
2. Turn and throw	Standing at a distance with back to partner	Both turn to right, throw and catch sock. Both turn to left and repeat	Feel tall, feet still, facing front. Arms straight	Back, waist
3. Pass over and under	Kneeling, knees apart with back to partner	Pass sock with two hands over head, return between knees. Watch sock throughout	Graceful stretch	Back, hips, thighs
4. Feet throw from sitting	Sitting facing at a a distance. Knees bent. Sock between feet	Throw sock with feet. Partner catches with hands	Sit tall. Long neck, chin in. Shoulders back	Waist, thighs
5. Throw between legs	Standing at a distance one behind the other. Feet apart	Partner with sock bends down and throws it between legs for partner to catch	Relaxed and balanced	Back, hips
6. Throw over head	As for Exercise 5	Partner with sock stretches up and throws sock over head to partner	As for Exercise 4	

COURSE C SET VI Exercises for extremities – long sitting

Name	Starting Position	Movement	Poise	To Improve
1. Foot circling	Long sitting	Toes up, out and down. Circle feet	Sit tall	Feet, ankles, calves
2. Head circling	As for Exercise 1	Head circling, slowly. Change direction	As for Exercise 1	Neck
3. Wrist circling. Stretch fingers	As for Exercise 1	Elbows bent but touching sides. Circle wrist (10) Clench fists and stretch fingers (10)	As for Exercise 1	Hands, wrists, forearm
4. Faces	Long sitting	With eyes and mouth exaggerate EE, OO, then squeeze face, relax, smile. Repeat	Sit tall	Facial and chin muscles
5. Shoulder roll	As for Exercise 4	Lift shoulders to ears and circle up back and down 10 times	As for Exercise 4	Neck, shoulders, bust
6. Banging	As for Exercise 4	With clenched fist bang tummy, thighs, hips. Stop, relax, breathe deeply. Repeat	As for Exercise 4	Increasing circulation and disperse the fat

COURSE C SET VII   Floor exercises with heavy stockings

Name	Starting Position	Movement	Poise	To Improve
1. Cross over chest	Lying on floor on your back. Both arms out sideways holding heavy stockings	Lift arms, bend and cross over chest. Return to start	Lie flat. Straight spine	Bust, waist
2. Alternate arm push	Lying on floor on your back. Bent elbows, holding heavy stockings	Push alternate fists towards ceiling	As for Exercise 1	Bust, waist
3. Arms together and apart	As for Exercise 1	Lift both arms straight above chest and lower slowly sideways	As for Exercise 1	Bust, waist
4. Alternate arm stretch	Lying on floor. Arms at sides holding heavy stockings	Lift one arm behind head on to floor. Change arms slowly	Lie flat. Straight spine	Bust, waist
5. Back arch	Lying on tummy arms at sides holding heavy stockings	Arch back, arms lift behind	Lying stretched	Back, hips
6. Semicircle arm stretch	As for Exercise 5	Lift arms, circle slowly sideways, stretch out in front of head. Rest. Lift and Return. Rest	As for Exercise 5	Back, hips

COURSE C SET VIII   Leg exercises with heavy stockings

Name	Starting Position	Movement	Poise	To Improve
1. One knee bend	Lying flat on back. Stockings tied round ankles and ball of foot	Bend right knee on to chest and lower to floor. Repeat alternate legs	Straight spine. Chin in.	Tummy and thighs
2. Straight leg cross over	Lying flat on back. Arms out sideways	Keeping shoulders on floor lift straight right leg and cross over left. Alternate legs	As for Exercise 1	Waist, hips
3. Side leg lift and pull	Lying on side supported by elbow and hand	Lift leg sideways up and pull with free hand. Lower slowly. Change sides and repeat	Shoulders back. Long neck	Waist, hips, thighs
4. Back leg circling	Lying on tummy. Hands on floor under forehead	Lift leg and circle in air. Repeat alternate legs	Straight and stretched	Back hips
5. Side leg circling	Lying on side supported by elbow and hand	Lift leg sideways and circle in air. Change sides and repeat	As for Exercise 4	Waist, hips, thighs
6. Knees bend and stretch	Lying on back knees bent, feet on floor. Arms by sides	Bend both knees to chest. Stretch feet up to ceiling. Bend to chest and back to start	Straight spine. Long neck	Tummy, thighs

COURSE C SET IX Arm exercises with heavy stockings

Name	Starting Position	Movement	Poise	To Improve
1. Arms circling	Standing with feet apart. Arms at sides. Heavy stockings held in hands	Lift arms out sideways. Circle forwards, up and back	Stand tall. Long neck. Seat tucked under	Bust, back
2. Shoulders lift up and down	As for Exercise 1	Lift shoulders up to ears and lower	As for Exercise 1	Shoulders
3. Arms crossed and stretched sideways	Stoop standing. Arms hanging down	Cross arms and fling open sideways. Repeat	Straight spine. Long neck	Back
4. Alternate arm reach high	Standing feet apart. Elbows bent	Look up and straighten alternate arms and reach towards ceiling	Standing tall	Back, waist
5. Arms raise sideways	Standing feet apart. Arms by sides	Lift both arms out sideways above head. Lower out sideways and down	As for Exercise 4	Trunk
6. Alternate arm reach forward	As for Exercise 4	Reach forward straightening alternate arms	As for Exercise 4	Bust, back

COURSE C SET X Exercises with heavy sock

Name	Starting Position	Movement	Poise	To Improve
1. Drop sock, twist and pick up	Standing feet together. Heavy sock in both hands. Straight arms	Raise arms above head. Look at sock. Drop behind. Bend knees, twist and pick up. Alternate sides	Stretched and relaxed	Waist, hips
2. Drop sock, pick up through legs	Standing feet apart. Straight arms holding sock	Lift arms above head. Drop sock behind. Keeping legs straight pick up between legs	As for Exercise 1	Back, waist, thighs
3. Drop sock and pick up facing front	As for Exercise 1	Lift arms above head. Drop sock behind. Bend knees facing front, reach for sock	As for Exercise 1	Waist, hips, thighs
4. Jump on spot	Standing, holding sock between feet	Jump up and down	Stretched and relaxed	Circulation
5. Overhead throw	Standing feet apart. Heavy sock in one hand	Throw sock sideways over head. Catch with other hand	Graceful	Bust, waist
6. Drop and catch	Standing feet together. Arms outstretched. Holding sock with both hands	Drop sock. Quickly bend both knees and catch it before it reaches the floor	Stand tall. Shoulders down and back	Hips, legs

COURSE D SET I Warm-up exercises

Name	Starting Position	Movement	Poise	To Improve
1. Walking	Standing. Feet together. Arms by sides	Slow walking on spot. Relaxed arm swing. Point raised foot	Head up. Long neck. Chin in. Chest out. Seat tucked under	General
2. Marching	As for Exercise 1	Marching on spot. Straight arm swing. Raise knee to hip level. Point toe	As for Exercise 1	General
3. High knee hold	As for Exercise 1	Raise alternate knees to chest level. Hold 3 secs. Point toe	As for Exercise 1	Back, thighs, legs
4. Running	Standing. Feet together. Arms by sides	Running on spot. Relaxed arms. Spring off ball of foot. Point toe	Long neck. Head up. Shoulders back. Seat tucked under	General
5. Running knees up	As for Exercise 4	Running on spot. Lift knee to hip level	As for Exercise 4	General
6. High knee running	As for Exercise 4	As for Exercise 5 with knees raised to waist level	As for Exercise 4	General

COURSE D SET II   Floor exercises – sitting

Name	Starting Position	Movement	Poise	To Improve
1. Sitting alternate high kick	Sitting knees bent. Feet off floor	Kick alternate leg up high	Balanced curve	Tummy, hips, thighs
2. Hips raise with bent leg cross over	Long sitting	Lift hips. Bend knee, cross over straight leg. Touch floor	Straight from head to toe	Back, hips, legs
3. Straight leg cross over	As for Exercise 2	Cross right leg over left. Lean to left. Repeat alternate legs. Shoulders to front	Straight back	Waist, legs
4. Touching toes	Long sitting. Legs apart. Hands on floor behind hips	Touch right foot with left hand, head on knee. Repeat alternate sides	Straight back and arms	Arms, back, waist, hips
5. Sit up touch toes	Lie on back. Legs together. Arms by sides	Sit up, hands off floor. Curl forward touch toes, head on knees. Uncurl	Straight spine on floor	Bust, waist, hips
6. Seat walking	Long sitting. Arms bent	Progress along floor on seat with bent arms used as in running	Sit tall	Back, waist, hips

COURSE D SET III Floor exercises – hands and knees

Name	Starting Position	Movement	Poise	To Improve
1. Back hump and arch	On hands and knees. Hands under shoulders, knees under hips	Hump back. Head between arms. Tuck seat under. Arch back	Head up. Chin in, long neck. Seat tucked under	Bust, waist, hips
2. Hip twist	As for Exercise 1	Twist hips to right. Turn head and look at right hip. Repeat other side	As for Exercise 1	Waist, hips
3. Waist circling	As for Exercise 1	Hump back, side, arch back, other side. Change direction	As for Exercise 1	Waist, hips
4. Knee bend under and stretch	On hands and knees. Hands under shoulders, knees under hips	Bend right knee to touch forehead. Right leg behind. Arch back	Head up. Chin in. Long neck. Seat tucked under	Waist, hips
5. Press forwards and rock backwards	As for Exercise 4	Lie flat by moving body forwards. Back to start. Sit on heels, head on floor	As for Exercise 4	General
6. Hip high and lower	As for Exercise 4 but toes tucked under	Raise hips, straighten legs. Lower hips. Hands and feet still. Head up	As for Exercise 4	Waist, hips, legs

COURSE D SET IV   Standing exercises with stick

Name	Starting Position	Movement	Poise	To Improve
1. Head level stick rotation	Standing feet apart holding stick at each end	Stick at head leve twist side to side looking backwards each time	Stand tall. Feet facing front. Long neck. Head up	Shoulders, waist, hips
2. Side bending	As for Exercise 1 holding stick behind head	Bend to alternate sides, shoulders facing front	As for Exercise 1	Waist
3. Stoop, stretch	Stoop standing, feet apart. Arms hanging down. Hold stick	Raise arms. Arch back. Lift head. Touch toes. head in	Long neck. Shoulders down. Long back	Back
4. Half circle swing	Stoop standing, legs apart. Arms hanging down. Hold stick	Relaxed knees. Swing stick upwards from side to side, keep head central	Long neck. Relaxed shoulders	Back, bust, waist
5. Bending facing partner	Long sitting facing partner. Legs apart. Feet touching. Holding one stick	Push and pull facing partner, holding stick	Head up. Long neck. Straight back	Back, bust, waist
6. Side rock facing partner	As for Exercise 5	Turn stick and bend to alternate sides following partner	As for Exercise 5	Waist, hips

COURSE D SET V Exercise with partner, using heavy sock

Name	Starting Position	Movement	Poise	To Improve
1. Under leg throw	Standing at a distance facing partner	Lift one leg and throw sock to partner under leg. Use alternate legs	Balanced and tall	Waist, hips, thighs
2. Turn and throw	Standing at a distance with back to partner	Both turn to right, throw and catch sock. Both turn to left and repeat	Feel tall, feet still, facing front. Arms straight	Back, waist
3. Pass over and under	Kneeling, knees apart with back to partner	Pass sock with two hands over head, return between knees. Watch sock	Graceful stretch	Back, hips, thighs
4. Feet throw from sitting	Sitting facing at a distance. Knees bent. Sock between feet	Throw sock with feet. Partner catches with hands	Sit tall. Chin in. Shoulders back	Waist, thighs
5. Feet throw behind	Standing at a distance one behind the other. Place sock between feet	Throw sock to partner from behind. Accuracy is your aim	As for Exercise 1	Back, hips
6. Feet throw from standing	Standing at a short distance facing partner. Sock between feet	Jump, knees up, and throw sock to partner. Swing arms up	Feel stretched	General

COURSE D SET VI Exercises for extremities – long sitting

Name	Starting Position	Movement	Poise	To Improve
1. Foot circling	Long sitting	Toes up, out and down. Circle feet	Sit tall	Feet, ankles, calves
2. Head circling	As for Exercise 1	Head circling, slowly. Change direction	As for Exercise 1	Neck
3. Wrist circling. Stretch fingers	As for Exercise 1	Elbows bent but touching sides. Circle wrist (10) Clench fists and stretch fingers (10)	As for Exercise 1	Hands, wrists, forearm
4. Faces	Long sitting	With eyes and mouth exaggerate EE and OO, then squeeze face, relax, smile. Repeat	Sit tall	Facial and chin muscles
5. Shoulder roll	As for Exercise 4	Lift shoulders to ears and circle up back and down 10 times	As for Exercise 4	Neck, shoulders, bust
6. Banging	As for Exercise 4	With clenched fist bang tummy, thighs, hips. Stop, relax, breathe deeply. Repeat	As for Exercise 4	Increasing circulation and disperse the fat

COURSE D SET VII Floor exercises with heavy stockings

Name	Starting Position	Movement	Poise	To Improve
1. Cross over chest	Lying on floor on your back. Both arms out sideways holding heavy stockings	Lift arms, bend and cross over chest. Return to start	Lie flat. Straight spine	Bust, waist
2. Alternate arm push	Lying on floor on your back. Bent elbows, holding heavy stockings	Push alternate fists towards ceiling	As for Exercise 1	Bust, waist
3. Arms together and apart	As for Exercise 1	Lift both arms straight above chest and lower slowly sideways	As for Exercise 1	Bust, waist
4. Alternate arm stretch	Lying on floor. Arms at sides holding heavy stockings	Lift one arm behind head on to floor. Change arms slowly	Lie flat. Straight spine	Bust, waist
5. Back arch	Lying on tummy arms at sides holding heavy stockings	Arch back, arms lift behind	Lying stretched	Back hips
6. Semi-circle arm stretch	As for Exercise 5	Lift arms, circle slowly sideways, stretch out in front of head. Rest. Lift. Return. Rest.	As for Exercise 5	Back, hips

COURSE D SET VIII Leg exercises with heavy stockings

Name	Starting Position	Movement	Poise	To Improve
1. One knee bend	Lying flat on back. Stockings tied round ankles and ball of foot	Bend right knee on to chest and lower to floor. Repeat alternate legs	Straight spine. Chin in	Waist, thighs
2. Straight leg cross over	Lying flat on back. Arms out sideways	Keeping shoulders on floor lift straight right leg, cross over left. Alternate legs	As for Exercise 1	Waist, hips
3. Side leg lift and pull	Lying on side supported by elbow and hand	Lift leg sideways up and pull with free hand. Lower slowly. Change sides and repeat	Shoulders back. Long neck.	Waist, hips, thighs
4. Back leg circling	Lying on tummy. Hands on floor under forehead	Lift leg and circle in air. Repeat alternate legs	Straight and stretched	Back, hips
5. Side leg circling	Lying on side supported by elbow and hand	Lift leg sideways and circle in air. Change sides and repeat	As for Exericse 4	Waist, hips thighs
6. Knees bend and stretch	Lying on back knees bent, feet on floor. Arms by sides	Bend both knees to chest. Stretch feet up to ceiling. Bend to chest and back to start	Straight spine. Long neck	Waist, thighs

R-S-G

COURSE D SET IX Arm exercises with heavy stockings

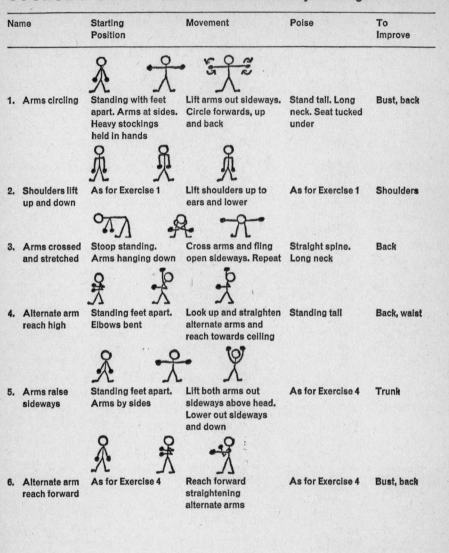

Name	Starting Position	Movement	Poise	To Improve
1. Arms circling	Standing with feet apart. Arms at sides. Heavy stockings held in hands	Lift arms out sideways. Circle forwards, up and back	Stand tall. Long neck. Seat tucked under	Bust, back
2. Shoulders lift up and down	As for Exercise 1	Lift shoulders up to ears and lower	As for Exercise 1	Shoulders
3. Arms crossed and stretched	Stoop standing. Arms hanging down	Cross arms and fling open sideways. Repeat	Straight spine. Long neck	Back
4. Alternate arm reach high	Standing feet apart. Elbows bent	Look up and straighten alternate arms and reach towards ceiling	Standing tall	Back, waist
5. Arms raise sideways	Standing feet apart. Arms by sides	Lift both arms out sideways above head. Lower out sideways and down	As for Exercise 4	Trunk
6. Alternate arm reach forward	As for Exercise 4	Reach forward straightening alternate arms	As for Exercise 4	Bust, back

COURSE D SET X Exercises with heavy sock

Name	Starting Position	Movement	Poise	To Improve
1. Drop sock, twist and pick up	Standing feet together. Heavy sock in both hands. Straight arms	Raise arms above head. Look at sock. Drop behind. Bend knees, twist and pick up. Alternate sides	Stretched and relaxed	Waist, hips
2. Drop sock, pick up through legs	Standing feet apart. Straight arms, holding sock	Lift arms above head. Drop sock behind. Keeping legs straight pick up between legs	As for Exercise 1	Back, waist, thighs
3. Drop sock and pick up facing front	As for Exercise 1	Lift arms above head. Drop sock behind. Bend knees facing front, reach for sock	As for Exercise 1	Waist, hips, thighs
4. Jump on spot	Standing, holding sock between feet	Jump up and down	Stretched and relaxed	Circulation
5. Overhead throw	Standing feet apart. Heavy sock in one hand	Throw sock sideways over head. Catch with other hand	Graceful	Bust, waist
6. Curl and straighten	Lying on back, sock in both hands	Sit up. Put sock between feet. Lie down, lift both feet. Pass sock to hands. Return feet to floor	As for Exercise 4	Waist

COURSE D SET XI Exercises with heavy sock

Name	Starting Position	Movement	Poise	To Improve
1. Straight leg lift	Standing feet together. Heavy sock balanced on top of one foot	Lift straight leg up and pass sock to hands. Repeat alternate legs	Stand tall. Shoulders back	Waist, hips, thighs
2. Diagonal pass behind back	Standing, feet apart. Sock in right hand	Pass sock over right shoulder to left hand behind back. Change arms	Stand tall. Tummy in. Seat under	Back, shoulder
3. Jump pass	Standing. Feet together. Sock in one hand	Jump high. Bend both knees. Pass sock under thighs from one hand to the other in the air	Stand tall ready to spring	Waist
4. Drop and catch	Standing feet together. Arms outstretched. Holding sock with both hands	Drop sock. Quickly bend both knees and catch it before it reaches the floor	Stand tall. Shoulders down and back	Hips, legs
5. Sit up from lying	Lying on back, hands holding sock under head	Keeping sock behind head, sit up, lie back	Shoulders back, long neck	Neck, waist, thighs
6. Hip roll	Lying on back. Sock between knees. Bend knees to chest	Roll knees from side to side touching floor keeping shoulders flat	Spine straight	Waist, hips

COURSE D SET XII General exercises

Name	Starting Position	Movement	Poise	To Improve
1. Bump and twist	Long sitting. Hands behind hips	Lift hips off floor. Bump up and down on seat and twist from side to side.	Sit tall	Hips, thighs
2. Leg circling in air	Lying on back	Raise hips and legs above shoulders. Elbows on floor hands supporting hips. Circling with legs	Stretched	Hips, legs
3. Side sit	Kneeling. Arms folded	Keeping arms folded sit on floor first to right side, up to kneeling and then to left	Long back	Waist, hips
4. Elbow press up	Lying on tummy, elbow and hands on floor. Toes tucked under	Lift hips off floor and lower. Make a straight line from head to toe	Straight spine	Back, waist, legs
5. Crouch jump	Knees bend, hands on floor, arms straight	Jump out, straight legs behind. Jump in to crouch	Hands under shoulders	General
6. Relaxed running on spot	Standing	Running on spot. Relaxed arms and legs	Relaxed	General

COURSE E SET I Warm-up exercises

Name	Starting Position	Movement	Poise	To Improve
1. Walking	Standing. Feet together. Arms by sides	Slow walking on spot. Relaxed arm swing. Point raised foot	Head up. Long neck. Chin in. Chest out. Seat tucked under	General
2. Marching	As for Exercise 1	Marching on spot. Straight arm swing. Raise knee to hip level. Point toe	As for Exercise 1	General
3. High knee hold	As for Exercise 1	Raise alternate knees to chest level. Hold 3 secs. Point toe	As for Exercise 1	Back, thighs, legs
4. Running	Standing. Feet together. Arms by sides	Running on spot. Relaxed arms. Spring off ball of foot. Point toe	Long neck. Head up. Shoulders back. Seat tucked under	General
5. Running knees up	As for Exercise 4	Running on spot. Lift knee to hip level	As for Exercise 4	General
6. High knee running	As for Exercise 4	As for Exercise 5 with knees raised to waist level	As for Exercise 4	General

COURSE E SET II Floor exercises – sitting

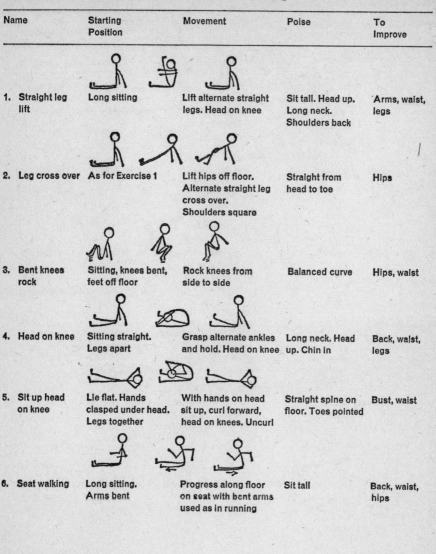

Name	Starting Position	Movement	Poise	To Improve
1. Straight leg lift	Long sitting	Lift alternate straight legs. Head on knee	Sit tall. Head up. Long neck. Shoulders back	Arms, waist, legs
2. Leg cross over	As for Exercise 1	Lift hips off floor. Alternate straight leg cross over. Shoulders square	Straight from head to toe	Hips
3. Bent knees rock	Sitting, knees bent, feet off floor	Rock knees from side to side	Balanced curve	Hips, waist
4. Head on knee	Sitting straight. Legs apart	Grasp alternate ankles and hold. Head on knee	Long neck. Head up. Chin in	Back, waist, legs
5. Sit up head on knee	Lie flat. Hands clasped under head. Legs together	With hands on head sit up, curl forward, head on knees. Uncurl	Straight spine on floor. Toes pointed	Bust, waist
6. Seat walking	Long sitting. Arms bent	Progress along floor on seat with bent arms used as in running	Sit tall	Back, waist, hips

COURSE E SET III Floor exercises – hands and knees

Name	Starting Position	Movement	Poise	To Improve
1. Back hump and arch	On hands and knees. Hands under shoulders, knees under hips	Hump back. Head between arms. Tuck seat under. Arch back	Head up. Chin in, long neck. Seat tucked under	Bust, waist, hips
2. Hip twist	As for Exercise 1	Twist hips to right. Turn head and look at right hip. Repeat other side	As for Exercise 1	Waist, hips
3. Waist circling	As for Exercise 1	Hump back, side, arch back, other side. Change direction	As for Exercise 1	Waist, hips
4. Knee bend under and stretch	On hands and knees. Hands under shoulders, knees under hips	Bend right knee to touch forehead. Stretch right leg behind. Arch back. Head up	Head up. Chin in, long neck. Seat tucked under	Waist, hips
5. Press forwards and rock backwards	As for Exercise 4	Lie flat by moving body forwards. Back to start. Sit on heels, head on floor	As for Exercise 4	General
6. Hip high and lower	As for Exercise 4 but toes tucked under	Raise hips, straighten legs. Lower hips. Hands and feet still. Head up	As for Exercise 4	Arms, waist, hips, legs

COURSE E SET IV Standing exercises with stick

Name	Starting Position	Movement	Poise	To Improve

1. Head to waist stick rotation	Standing feet apart holding stick at each end	Holding stick at head level, twist down to waist level and back. Turn head. Alternate sides	Stand tall. Feet facing front. Head up.	Waist, hips
2. Side bending	As for Exercise 1 holding stick above head	Bend to alternate sides, shoulders facing front	As for Exercise 1	Waist
3. Stoop, stretch	Stoop standing, feet apart. Arms hanging down straight, hold stick	Raise arms. Arch back, stick behind head, stretch arms. Touch toes	Long back. Braced legs	Back, hips legs
4. Half circle swing	Stoop standing, legs apart. Arms hanging down. Hands hold stick	Relaxed knees. Swing stick upwards from side to side, keep head central	Long neck. Relaxed shoulders	Arms, back, bust, waist
5. Bending facing partner	Long sitting facing partner. Legs apart feet touching. Holding one stick	Push and pull facing partner, holding stick	Head up. Long neck. Straight back	Back, bust, waist
6. Side rock facing partner	As for Exercise 5	Turn stick and bend to alternate sides following partner	As for Exercise 5	Waist, hips

COURSE E SET V Exercises with partner, using heavy socks

Name	Starting Position	Movement	Poise	To Improve
1. Under leg throw, 2 socks	Standing at a distance facing partner	Both lift one leg and throw sock under leg to partner. Use alternate legs	Balanced and tall	Waist, hips, thighs
2. Turn and throw with 2 socks	Standing at a distance with back to partner	Both turn to right, throw and exchange socks. Both turn to left and repeat	Feet still facing front. Arms straight	Back, waist
3. Pass over and under with 1 sock	Standing at a distance with back to partner	Throw sock gently overhead. Partner catches it in back bend position and returns through legs	Balanced and graceful	Back, waist, hips, thighs
4. Sitting feet throw	Sitting at a distance facing. Each place sock between feet	Lean back. Throw and exchange socks	Sit tall. Chin in. Shoulders back	Waist, thighs
5. Two feet throw from behind	Standing at a distance one behind the other. Sock between feet of front partner	Jump and throw sock behind to partner who turns round to repeat	As for Exercise 1	Back, hips, thighs
6. Feet throw from standing	Standing facing partner. Each holds sock between feet	Jump, knees up, throw and exchange socks. Swing arms up	Feel stretched	General

COURSE E SET VI Exercises for extremities – long sitting

Name	Starting Position	Movement	Poise	To Improve
1. Foot circling	Long sitting	Toes up, out and down. Circle feet	Sit tall	Feet ankles, calves
2. Head circling	As for Exercise 1	Head circling, slowly. Change direction	As for Exercise 1	Neck
3. Wrist circling. Stretch fingers	As for Exercise 1	Elbows bent touching sides. Circle wrist (10), clench fists and stretch fingers (10)	As for Exercise 1	Hands, wrists, forearm
4. Faces	Long sitting	With eyes and mouth exaggerate EE, OO, then squeeze face, relax, smile. Repeat	Sit tall	Facial and chin muscles
5. Shoulder roll	As for Exercise 4	Lift shoulders to ears and circle up back and down 10 times	As for Exercise 4	Neck, shoulders, bust
6. Banging	As for Exercise 4	With clenched fist bang tummy, thighs, hips. Stop, relax, breathe deeply. Repeat	As for Exercise 4	Increasing circulation and disperse the fat

COURSE E SET VII Exercises with heavy stockings

Name	Starting Position	Movement	Poise	To Improve
1. Cross over chest	Lying on floor on your back. Both arms out sideways holding heavy stockings	Lift arms, bend and cross over chest. Return to start	Lie flat. Straight spine	Bust, waist
2. Alternate arm push	Lying on floor on your back. Bent elbows holding heavy stockings	Push alternate fists towards ceiling	As for Exercise 1	Bust, waist
3. Arms together and apart	As for Exercise 1	Lift both arms straight above chest and lower slowly sideways	As for Exercise 1	Bust, waist
4. Alternate arm stretch	Lying on floor. Arms at sides holding heavy stockings	Lift one arm behind head on to floor. Change arms slowly	Lie flat. Straight spine	Bust, waist
5. Back arch	Lying on tummy arms at sides holding heavy stockings	Arch back, arms lift behind	Lying stretched	Back, hips
6. Semi-circle arm stretch	As for Exercise 5	Lift arms, circle slowly sideways, stretch out in front of head. Rest. Return. Rest	As for Exercise 5	Back, hips

COURSE E SET VIII Leg exercises with heavy stockings

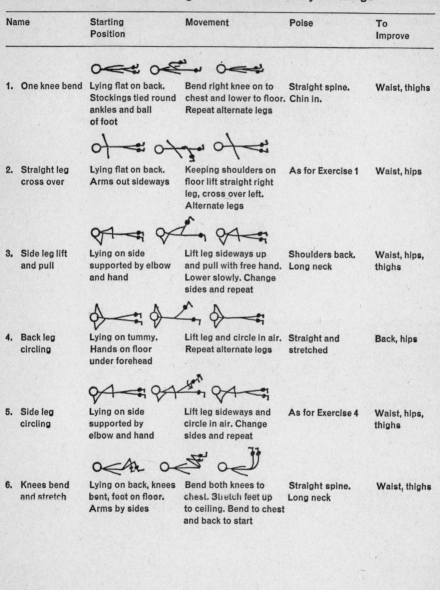

Name	Starting Position	Movement	Poise	To Improve
1. One knee bend	Lying flat on back. Stockings tied round ankles and ball of foot	Bend right knee on to chest and lower to floor. Repeat alternate legs	Straight spine. Chin in.	Waist, thighs
2. Straight leg cross over	Lying flat on back. Arms out sideways	Keeping shoulders on floor lift straight right leg, cross over left. Alternate legs	As for Exercise 1	Waist, hips
3. Side leg lift and pull	Lying on side supported by elbow and hand	Lift leg sideways up and pull with free hand. Lower slowly. Change sides and repeat	Shoulders back. Long neck	Waist, hips, thighs
4. Back leg circling	Lying on tummy. Hands on floor under forehead	Lift leg and circle in air. Repeat alternate legs	Straight and stretched	Back, hips
5. Side leg circling	Lying on side supported by elbow and hand	Lift leg sideways and circle in air. Change sides and repeat	As for Exercise 4	Waist, hips, thighs
6. Knees bend and stretch	Lying on back, knees bent, foot on floor. Arms by sides	Bend both knees to chest. Stretch feet up to ceiling. Bend to chest and back to start	Straight spine. Long neck	Waist, thighs

COURSE E SET IX   Arm exercises with heavy stockings

Name	Starting Position	Movement	Poise	To Improve
1. Arms circling	Standing with feet apart. Arms at sides. Heavy stockings held in hands	Lift arms out sideways. Circle forwards, up and back	Stand tall. Long neck. Seat tucked under	Bust, back
2. Shoulders lift up and down	As for Exercise 1	Lift shoulders up to ears and lower	As for Exercise 1	Shoulders
3. Arms crossed and stretched	Stoop standing. Arms hanging down	Cross arms and fling open sideways. Repeat	Straight spine. Long neck	Back
4. Alternate arm reach high	Standing feet apart. Elbows bent	Look up and straighten alternate arms and reach towards ceiling	Standing tall	Back, waist
5. Arms raise sideways	Standing feet apart. Arms by sides	Lift both arms out sideways above head. Lower out sideways and down	As for Exercise 4	Trunk
6. Alternate arm reach forward	As for Exercise 4	Reach forward straightening alternate arms	As for Exercise 4	Bust, back

COURSE E SET X Exercises with heavy sock

Name	Starting Position	Movement	Poise	To Improve
1. Drop sock, twist and pick up	Standing feet together. Heavy sock in both hands	Raise arms above head. Look at sock. Drop behind. Bend knees, twist and pick up. Alternate sides	Stretched and relaxed	Waist, hips
2. Drop sock, pick up through legs	Standing feet apart. Straight arms, holding sock	Lift arms above head. Drop sock behind. Keeping legs straight pick up between legs	As for Exercise 1	Back, waist, thighs
3. Drop sock and pick up facing front	As for Exercise 1	Lift arms above head. Drop sock behind. Bend knees facing front, reach for sock	As for Exercise 1	Waist, hips, thighs
4. Jump on spot	Standing, holding sock between feet	Jump up and down	Stretched and relaxed	Circulation
5. Overhead throw	Standing feet apart. Heavy sock in one hand	Throw sock sideways over head. Catch with other hand	Graceful	Bust, waist
6. Curl and straighten	Lying on back, sock in both hands	Sit up. Put sock between feet. Lie down, lift both feet. Pass sock to hands. Return feet to floor	As for Exercise 4	Waist

COURSE E SET XI Exercises with heavy sock

Name	Starting Position	Movement	Poise	To Improve
1. Straight leg lift	Standing feet together. Heavy sock balanced on top of one foot	Lift straight leg up and pass sock to hands. Repeat alternate legs	Stand tall. Shoulders back	Waist, hips, thighs
2. Diagonal pass behind back	Standing, feet apart. Sock in right hand	Pass sock over right shoulder to left hand behind back. Change arms	Stand tall. Tummy in. Seat under	Back, shoulders
3. Jump pass	Standing. Feet together. Sock in one hand	Jump high. Bend both knees. Pass sock under thighs from one hand to the other in the air	Stand tall ready to spring	Waist
4. Drop and catch	Standing feet together. Arms outstretched. Holding sock with both hands	Drop sock. Quickly bend both knees and catch it before it reaches the floor	Stand tall. Shoulders down and back	Hips, legs
5. Sit up from lying	Lying on back, hands holding sock under head	Keeping sock behind head, sit up, lie back	Shoulders back, long neck	Neck, waist, thighs
6. Hip roll	Lying on back. Sock between knees. Bend knees to chest	Roll knees from side to side touching floor keeping shoulders flat	Spine straight	Waist, hips

COURSE E SET XII General exercises

Name	Starting Position	Movement	Poise	To Improve

1. Bump and twist	Long sitting. Hands behind hips	Lift hips off floor. Bump up and down on seat and twist from side to side	Sit tall	Hips, thighs
2. Leg circling in air	Lying on back	Raise hips and legs above shoulders. Elbows on floor, hands supporting hips. Circling with legs	Stretched	Hips, legs
3. Sit side to side	Kneeling. Arms folded	Keeping arms folded sit on floor first to right side, up to kneeling and then to left	Long back	Waist, hips
4. Elbow press up	Lying on tummy. Elbows and hands on floor. Toes tucked under	Lift hips off floor and lower. Make a straight line from head to toe	Straight spine	Back, waist, legs
5. Crouch jump	Knees bend, hands on floor, arms straight	Jump out, straight legs behind. Jump in to crouch	Hands under shoulders	General
6. Relaxed running on spot	Standing	Running on spot. Floppy arms and legs	Relaxed	General

R–S–H

COURSE F SET I Warm-up exercises

Name	Starting Position	Movement	Poise	To Improve
1. Walking	Standing. Feet together. Arms by sides	Slow walking on spot. Relaxed arm swing. Point raised foot	Head up. Long neck. Chin in. Chest out. Seat tucked under	General
2. Marching	As for Exercise 1	Marching on spot. Straight arm swing. Raise knee to hip level. Point toe	As for Exercise 1	General
3. High knee hold	As for Exercise 1	Raise alternate knees to chest level. Hold 3 secs. Point toe	As for Exercise 1	Back, thighs, legs
4. Running	Standing. Feet together. Arms by sides	Running on spot. Relaxed arms. Spring off ball of foot. Point toe	Long neck. Head up. Shoulders back. Seat tucked under	General
5. Running knees up	As for Exercise 1	Running on spot. Lift knee to hip level	As for Exercise 4	General
6. High knee running	As for Exercise 1	As for Exercise 5 with knees raised to waist level	As for Exercise 4	General

COURSE F SET II Floor exercises – sitting

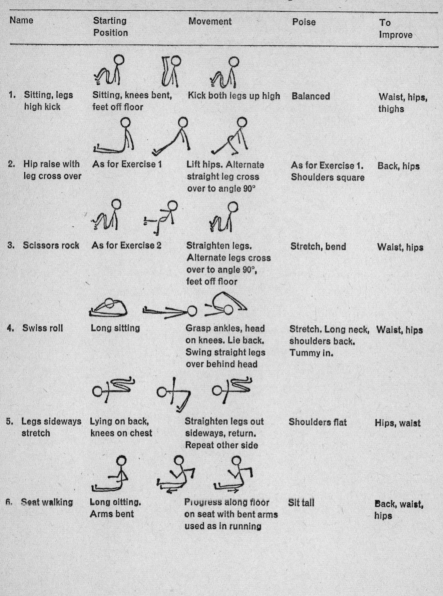

Name	Starting Position	Movement	Poise	To Improve
1. Sitting, legs high kick	Sitting, knees bent, feet off floor	Kick both legs up high	Balanced	Waist, hips, thighs
2. Hip raise with leg cross over	As for Exercise 1	Lift hips. Alternate straight leg cross over to angle 90°	As for Exercise 1. Shoulders square	Back, hips
3. Scissors rock	As for Exercise 2	Straighten legs. Alternate legs cross over to angle 90°, feet off floor	Stretch, bend	Waist, hips
4. Swiss roll	Long sitting	Grasp ankles, head on knees. Lie back. Swing straight legs over behind head	Stretch. Long neck, shoulders back. Tummy in.	Waist, hips
5. Legs sideways stretch	Lying on back, knees on chest	Straighten legs out sideways, return. Repeat other side	Shoulders flat	Hips, waist
6. Seat walking	Long sitting. Arms bent	Progress along floor on seat with bent arms used as in running	Sit tall	Back, waist, hips

COURSE F SET III Floor exercises – hands and knees

Name	Starting Position	Movement	Poise	To Improve
1. Back hump and arch	On hands and knees. Hands under shoulders, knees under hips	Hump back. Head between arms. Tuck seat under. Arch back	Head up. Chin in, long neck. Seat tucked under	Bust waist, hips
2. Hip twist	As for Exercise 1	Twist hips to right. Turn head and look at right hip. Repeat other side	As for Exercise 1	Waist, hips
3. Waist circling	As for Exercise 1	Hump back, side, arch back, other side. Change direction	As for Exercise 1	Waist, hips
4. Knee bend under and stretch	On hands and knees. Hands under shoulders, knees under hips	Bend right knee to touch forehead. Stretch right leg behind. Arch back. Head up	Head up. Chin in, long neck. Seat tucked in	Waist, hips
5. Press forwards and rock backwards	As for Exercise 4	Lie flat by moving body forwards. Back to start. Sit on heels, head on floor	As for Exercise 4	General
6. Hip high and lower	As for Exercise 4 but toes tucked under	Raise hips, straighten legs. Lower hips. Hands and feet still. Head up	As for Exercise 1	Arms, waist, hips, legs

COURSE F SET IV Standing exercises with stick

Name	Starting Position	Movement	Poise	To Improve
1. Head to knee stick rotation	Standing feet apart holding stick at each end	Stick at head level, twist down to knee level and back. Alternate sides. Turn head.	Stand tall. Feet facing front. Head up	Shoulders, arms, waist, thighs
2. Side bending	As for Exercise 1 holding stick above head	Bend to alternate sides shoulders facing front. Reach to knee on each side	As for Exercise 1	Waist
3. Stoop, stretch, stick behind head	Stoop standing. Feet apart. Arms hanging down. Hands hold stick	Stick behind shoulders. Stretch arms. Touch toes.	Long back. Braced legs	Back, hips
4. Half circle swing	Stoop, standing straight legs apart. Arms hang down holding stick	Relaxed knees. Swing stick upwards from side to side, keep head central	Long neck. Relaxed shoulders	Back, bust, waist
5. Round-about	Long sitting facing partner, legs apart, feet touching. Holding stick	Push forwards, sideways pull backwards, sideways. Round and round. Change direction	Head up. Back straight	Waist, hips
6. Pull over partner	Sitting back to back legs together knees bent. Hold stick high above head	Gently lean forwards and pull your partner onto your back. Partner lifts hips and stretches	Straight backs. Heads up	Bust, waist, legs

COURSE F SET V Exercises with partner, using heavy sock

Name	Starting Position	Movement	Poise	To Improve
1. Under leg throw, 2 socks	Standing at a distance facing partner	Both lift one leg and throw sock under leg to partner. Use alternate legs	Balanced and tall	Waist, hips, thighs
2. Turn and throw with 2 socks	Standing at a distance with back to back	Both turn to right, throw and exchange socks. Both turn to left and repeat	Feet still facing front. Arms straight	Back, waist
3. Pass over and under with 1 sock	Standing at a distance with back to partner	Throw sock gently overhead. Partner catches it in back bend position and returns through legs	Balanced and graceful	Back, waist, hips, thighs
4. Sitting feet throw	Sitting knees bent at a distance facing partner	Place sock between feet. Lean back. Throw and exchange	Sit tall. Chin in	Waist, thighs
5. Two feet throw from behind	Standing. Sock between feet of front partner	Jump and throw sock behind to partner, who turns round to repeat	As for Exercise 1	Back, hips, thighs
6. Feet throw from standing	Standing at a short distance facing partner. Each holds sock at feet	Jump, knees up, throw and exchange socks. Swing arms up	Feel stretched	General

COURSE F SET VII Exercises for extremities – long sitting

Name	Starting Position	Movement	Poise	To Improve
1. Foot circling	Long sitting	Toes up, out and down. Circle feet	Sit tall	Feet, ankles, calves
2. Head circling	As for Exercise 1	Head circling, slowly. Change direction	As for Exercise 1	Neck
3. Wrist circling stretch fingers	As for Exercise 1	Elbows bent but touching sides. Circle wrist (10) Clench fists and stretch fingers (10)	As for Exercise 1	Hands, wrists forearm
4. Faces	Long sitting	With eyes and mouth exaggerate EE, OO, then squeeze face, relax, smile. Repeat	Sit tall	Facial and chin muscles
5. Shoulder roll	As for Exercise 4	Lift shoulders to ears and circle up back and down 10 times	As for Exercise 4	Neck, shoulders, bust
6. Banging	As for Exercise 4	With clenched fist bang tummy, thighs, and hips. Stop, relax and breathe deeply. Repeat	As for Exercise 4	Increasing circulation and disperse the fat

COURSE F SET VII Exercises with heavy stockings

Name	Starting Position	Movement	Poise	To Improve
1. Cross over chest	Lying on floor on your back. Both arms out sideways holding heavy stockings	Lift arms, bend and cross over chest. Return to start	Lie flat. Straight spine	Bust, waist
2. Alternate arm push	Lying on floor on your back. Bent elbows, holding heavy stockings	Push alternate fists towards ceiling	As for Exercise 1	Bust, waist
3. Arms together and apart	As for Exercise 1	Lift both arms straight above chest and lower slowly sideways	As for Exercise 1	Bust, waist
4. Alternate arm stretch	Lying on floor. Arms at sides holding heavy stockings	Lift one arm behind head on to floor. Change arms slowly	Lie flat. Straight spine	Bust, waist
5. Back arch	Lying on tummy arms at sides holding heavy stockings	Arch back, arms lift behind	Lying stretched	Back, hips
6. Semicircle arm stretch	As for Exercise 5	Lift arms, circle slowly sideways, stretch out in front of head. Rest. Lift. Return. Rest	As for Exercise 5	Back, hips

COURSE F SET VIII   Leg exercises with heavy stockings

Name	Starting Position	Movement	Poise	To Improve
1. One knee bend	Lying flat on back. Stockings tied round ankles and ball of foot	Bend right knee on to chest, and lower to floor. Repeat alternate legs	Straight spine. Chin in	Thighs
2. Straight leg cross over	Lying flat on back. Arms out sideways	Keeping shoulders on floor lift straight right leg and cross over left. Alternate legs	As for Exercise 1	Waist, hips
3. Side leg lift and pull	Lying on side supported by elbow and hand	Lift leg sideways up and pull with free hand. Lower slowly. Change sides and repeat	Shoulders back. Long neck	Waist, hips, thighs
4. Back leg circling	Lying on tummy. Hands on floor under forehead	Lift leg and circle in air. Repeat alternate legs	Straight and stretched	Back, hips
5. Side leg circling	Lying on side supported by elbow and hand	Lift leg sideways and circle in air. Change sides and repeat	As for Exercise 4	Waist, hips, thighs
6. Knees bend and stretch	Lying on back, knees bent, feet on floor. Arms by sides	Bend both knees to chest. Stretch feet up to ceiling. Bend to chest and back to start	Straight spine. Long neck	Waist, thighs

COURSE F SET IX Arm exercises with heavy stockings

Name	Starting Position	Movement	Poise	To Improve
1. Arms circling	Standing with feet apart. Arms at sides. Heavy stockings held in hands	Lift arms out sideways. Circle forwards, up and back	Stand tall. Long neck. Seat tucked under	Bust, back
2. Shoulders lift up and down	As for Exercise 1	Lift shoulders up to ears and lower	As for Exercise 1	Shoulders
3. Arms crossed and stretched	Stoop standing. Arms hanging down	Cross and fling open sideways. Repeat	Straight spine. Long neck	Back
4. Alternate arm reach high	Standing feet apart. Elbows bent	Look up and straighten alternate arms and reach towards ceiling	Standing tall	Back, waist
5. Arms raise sideways	Standing feet apart. Arms by sides	Lift both arms out sideways above head. Lower out sideways and down	As for Exercise 4	Trunk
6. Alternate arm reach forward	As for Exercise 4	Reach forward straightening alternate arms	As for Exercise 4	Bust, back

COURSE F SET X Exercises with heavy sock

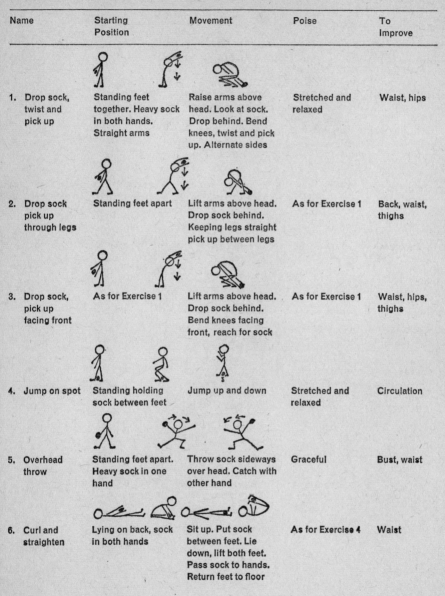

Name	Starting Position	Movement	Poise	To Improve
1. Drop sock, twist and pick up	Standing feet together. Heavy sock in both hands. Straight arms	Raise arms above head. Look at sock. Drop behind. Bend knees, twist and pick up. Alternate sides	Stretched and relaxed	Waist, hips
2. Drop sock pick up through legs	Standing feet apart	Lift arms above head. Drop sock behind. Keeping legs straight pick up between legs	As for Exercise 1	Back, waist, thighs
3. Drop sock, pick up facing front	As for Exercise 1	Lift arms above head. Drop sock behind. Bend knees facing front, reach for sock	As for Exercise 1	Waist, hips, thighs
4. Jump on spot	Standing holding sock between feet	Jump up and down	Stretched and relaxed	Circulation
5. Overhead throw	Standing feet apart. Heavy sock in one hand	Throw sock sideways over head. Catch with other hand	Graceful	Bust, waist
6. Curl and straighten	Lying on back, sock in both hands	Sit up. Put sock between feet. Lie down, lift both feet. Pass sock to hands. Return feet to floor	As for Exercise 4	Waist

COURSE F SET XI Exercises with heavy sock

Name	Starting Position	Movement	Poise	To Improve
1. Straight leg lift	Standing feet together. Heavy sock balanced on top of one foot	Lift straight leg up and pass sock to hands. Repeat alternate legs	Stand tall. Shoulders back	Waist, hips thighs
2. Diagonal pass behind back	Standing, feet apart. Sock in right hand	Pass sock over right shoulder to left hand behind back. Change arms	Stand tall. Tummy in. Seat under	Back, shoulders
3. Jump pass	Standing. Feet together. Sock in one hand	Jump high. Bend both knees. Pass sock under thighs from one hand to the other in the air	Stand tall ready to spring	Waist
4. Drop and catch	Standing feet together. Arms outstretched. Holding sock with both hands	Drop sock. Quickly bend both knees and catch it before it reaches the floor	Stand tall. Shoulders down and back	Hips, legs
5. Sit up from lying	Lying on back holding sock under head	Keeping sock behind head, sit up, lie back	Shoulders back, long neck	Neck, waist, thighs
6. Hip roll	Lying on back. Sock between knees. Bend knees to chest	Roll knees from side to side touching floor keeping shoulders flat	Spine straight	Waist, hips

COURSE F SET XII General exercises

Name	Starting Position	Movement	Poise	To Improve

1. Bump and twist	Long sitting. Hands behind hips	Lift hips off floor. Bump up and down on seat and twist from side to side	Sit tall	Hips, thighs
2. Leg circling In air	Lying on back	Raise hips and legs above shoulders. Elbows on floor, hands supporting hips. Circling with legs	Stretched	Hips, legs
3. Sit side to side	Kneeling. Arms folded	Keeping arms folded sit on floor first to right side, up to kneeling and then to left	Long back	Waist, hips
4. Elbow press up	Lying on tummy. Elbows and hands on floor. Toes tucked under	Lift hips off floor and lower. Make a straight line from head to toe	Straight spine	Back, waist, legs
5. Crouch jump	Knees bend, hands on floor, arms straight	Jump out, straight legs behind. Jump in to crouch	Hands under shoulders. Straight spine	General
6. Relaxed running on spot	Standing	Running on spot. Floppy arms and legs	Relax	General

OPTIONAL COMPETITIVE EXERCISES

Name	Starting Position	Movement	Poise	To Improve
1. Tug of war	Standing side by side. Hold right hands. Legs apart. Outsides of right feet touching	Pull away from each other. Repeat other side. To win pull your partner to your side	Stretched	General
2. Shoulder push	Standing facing partner. One foot in front of the other. Hands on shoulders	To win push partner away	Stand tall	General
3. Hold and hop	Standing facing partner. Hold foot with one hand and partner's hand with the other	Push and pull partner vigorously. Try to force partner to release foot	Arched and stretched	General
4. Touch below knee	Standing facing partner. Feet apart	Try to touch partner below knee while preventing her from touching you	Balanced	General
5. Crouch pull and push	Knees bent face partner, hands on each other's shoulders	Jump in squat position, pull and push. Try to unbalance partner	Straight back	General
6. Standing pull and push	Standing facing partner. Feet one in front of the other, toe touching heel	Hold partners hands. Pull and push trying to force partner to move feet	As for Exercise 5	General

More about Penguins

Penguinews, which appears every month, contains details of all the new books issued by Penguins as they are published. From time to time it is supplemented by *Penguins in Print*, which is a complete list of all books published by Penguins which are in print. (There are well over three thousand of these.)

A specimen copy of *Penguinews* will be sent to you free on request, and you can become a subscriber for the price of the postage. For a year's issues (including the complete lists) please send 30p if you live in the United Kingdom, or 60p if you live elsewhere. Just write to Dept EP, Penguin Books Ltd, Harmondsworth, Middlesex, enclosing a cheque or postal order, and your name will be added to the mailing list.

Note: *Penguinews* and *Penguins in Print* are not available in the U.S.A. or Canada

A Penguin Handbook

The Slimmer's Cook Book
J. Yudkin & G. M. Chappell

The best diet for slimming is also the best diet for health.
In this book Professor Yudkin, author of *This Slimming
Business*, and Professor of Nutrition and Dietetics at Queen
Elizabeth College, University of London, and Gweneth
M. Chappell, a senior lecturer in Household Science, present
the would-be slimmer with a selection of dishes which
ensure that he or she need never feel hungry. The
preparation of these is based on the principle of cutting
down as much as possible on the intake of carbohydrates,
replacing them with meat, fish, eggs, and all the other
protein-giving foods. Contrary to popular belief, the cost of
these foods is not prohibitive: a wide range of
inexpensive dishes is described. In addition to more simple
meals which can be prepared in a matter of minutes, there
are also many elaborate concoctions for social occasions,
suitable for slimmers and non-slimmers alike. A special
section on 'portable' low-carbohydrate meals is included
for those who daily take packed lunches to their place of
work. This new edition includes a valuable table of
carbohydrate units.

Also available
This Slimming Business by *John Yudkin*

Not for sale in the U.S.A. or Canada